A–Z
OF
DOG TRAINING
& BEHAVIOUR

Patrick Holden & Kay White

HOWELL
BOOK
HOUSE

New York

HOWELL
BOOK
HOUSE

HOWELL BOOK HOUSE
A Macmillan Company
1633 Broadway
New York, NY 10019

MACMILLAN is a registered trademark of Macmillan, Inc.

ISBN 1-58245-007-2

Library of Congress Cataloging-in-Publication Data
available on request

Printed in Hong Kong

10 9 8 7 6 5 4 3 2 1

CONTENTS

THE AUTHORS

Patrick Holden has been involved in dog training for over 25 years both training his own dogs, and others as an instructor. He is an Obedience Competition judge.

He trained his Labrador, Whisky, to be the highest qualifying Labrador in Obedience in the UK, and then trained his present Golden Retriever Ob. Ch. Melnola Bramble CDEX-TDEX as the first, and, so far, the only, Golden of all time to qualify at the topmost level in both Working Trials (TDEX) and Obedience (Obedience Champion). He has also trained Bramble to compete in Senior Agility in the Superdogs Final. They have been at Crufts together for several years in the teams and individual obedience finals.

In 1996 Bramble was the only, and in 1998 only one of two gundogs in the UK to qualify for the Crufts Individual Obedience Championship.

Patrick is now starting to train Bramble's son, Thorn, for competition.

Kay White has been entranced by dogs since early childhood. Her earliest memories are of Pekingese, then Airedales, and a bright, ginger-coloured cross-bred who came with Santa Claus one year. Marriage brought a red Cocker Spaniel and one of the early post-war Boxers. A move to the country made a dream come true – a boarding and breeding kennel. Kay specialised in Boxers, Cavalier King Charles Spaniels, and some black Great Danes.

The next major breakthrough came when she persuaded the Animal Health Trust, a pioneering centre of animal excellence known throughout the world, to host the first residential course for dog breeders, and so began a long campaign for breeder education which continues to this day.

Kay is a prolific writer on animal care and has co-written the best-selling books *Doglopaedia, Catlopaedia, and Book Of the Bitch* published by Ringpress Books in the UK and with Howell Book House in the USA.

SECTION I

PRINCIPLES
OF TRAINING

By Kay White

Chapter One

THE WOLF'S LEGACY

Nearly all pet dogs and most working dogs have altered their status enormously in the last few decades; they have literally come in from the cold to join us as valued members of our family, to share our home comforts, our pleasures and our relaxation – and often, our work too.

While inviting our dogs to live what is virtually a life of luxury, compared with the kennel or stable accommodation that was once their recognised environment, we have also largely deprived our dogs of the work they have been bred to do for thousands of years. Many breeds that were selectively bred for certain tasks, such as herding livestock, pulling small carts, hunting and pulling down their quarry or digging out vermin now find themselves completely idle, with no outlet for their developed talents. Where there is inherited working ability, long-term inactivity is not an easy adjustment to make for humans or animals.

In making this transition to indoor life, we have also sentenced dogs to learning a new language. We have done away with the crisp command and the code of whistles, to which their ancestors responded so readily, and we have substituted a soft-toned domestic whisper in a variable vocabulary, but we still expect immediate obedience. And along with this soft living, we provide better nutrition and more sophisticated veterinary care than dogs have ever known before.

No wonder dogs experience some problems in learning to live with us, and we, in our turn, may sometimes despair of ever reaching a rewarding level of understanding with our dogs. This book seeks to help owners to reach that mutual plane of affectionate understanding and tolerance with their dogs, with a lot of pleasure and as little stress as possible.

EVOLUTION

The evolution of the domestic dog began some 200 million years ago, but it was the extinction of the dinosaurs about 70 million years ago that gave the smaller mammals the opportunity to establish themselves. The miacids, small, long-bodied, meat-eating weasel-like creatures are thought to be the ancestors of all the dog-like species we know today. From the miacids sprang the miacines, and from them, the dogs, bears, raccoons, and regional varieties of wolf that are familiar to us today.

It is believed that when primitive man began to farm and to breed livestock 14,000 years ago, they probably deduced that the hunting behaviour shown by a wolf pack could be adapted to controlling and rounding up herds of other animals. The friendliest wolves from a pack were probably taken as young ones into the caves that were home to the humans, and the wolves were probably tamed by feeding treats, just as we do today.

The domestic dog belongs to the family *Canidae*, a classification which includes wolves, foxes, coyotes and jackals, as well as many other species. Our dogs are categorised as *Canis familiaris*, and are thought to have

*The dog has had to learn a new
language to fit in with domestic life.*

descended from varieties of wolves that were tamed, accidentally or intentionally, by primitive man. These tamed wolves were the precursors, by many thousands of years, of our domestic dogs, in which more than a little of the wolf characteristics still remain.

Wolves have been portrayed in folk stories and legends as being dangerous to man, but, in fact, they seldom kill unless attacked, and they hardly ever fight among themselves. Wolves usually mate for life and bring up their young with kindness and good humour; play is important to all the generations, just as it is to our dogs. Wolves live as a pack, usually ruled by an alpha male and an alpha female, who may be the only animals in the pack which mate and produce young.

A wolf pack is a highly integrated and caring family, very dependent on each other, especially when hunting for food. Hunting within a pack meant that wolves could pull down animals much larger than themselves, rather than being confined to the small prey which one animal alone could get.

Dogs have inherited this need for the support of a pack, and in the domestic world, we, the dog's owners, must provide that sympathetic but resolute framework of education and care which enables the dog to live contentedly in our home pack.

Archaeologists believe that dogs were the first animal species to be domesticated, and that the canine race achieved this status when human survival still depended on hunting and foraging, because dogs proved themselves so useful when they co-operated in the chase and the kill.

INHERITED TRAITS

What are the wolf traits that our dogs have inherited? In many ways, every dog, from the smallest to the largest, shows wolf-derived behaviour every day of his life, although we try to prevent dogs showing those traits that we are not comfortable living with.

Wolves mark their territory through the scent glands in their paws, and also by deliberate urination at certain marker points. Our dogs and bitches regard urine marking as an essential duty in their day. Dogs roll in manure heaps, or where other livestock has been, to cover up their own scent. Dogs want to jump up and lick our faces, just as puppies and wolf cubs lick the mouth of their dam to persuade her to regurgitate food for them. When adult dogs try to face and hand-lick when greeting people, it is regression to puppy

Left:
Photo: Carol Ann Johnson.

From the smallest to the largest, all dogs show wolf-related behaviour.

Below:
Photo: Sheila Atter.

behaviour, and probably a way of begging for acceptance.

Both dogs and wolves communicate between themselves and with humans by a variety of sounds, ranging from grunts, squeals, whines, barks and muffled growls, but the sound that wolves are most associated with is the group howl, often performed in the early morning or in the evening. A howl carries further than any other sound, and is used to communicate with other packs as well as to call in straying members of the home pack.

It is therefore not remarkable that a dog in the house will resort to howling when he is left alone, although he may

Most dogs spend their day in a light sleep, ready to be on the alert to any unfamiliar noise or movement.

Photo: Amanda Bulbeck.

never howl at any other time. Perhaps the dog's primitive instinct resurfaces when a dog finds itself bored and lonely.

Playing tugging games and burying things, digging and tracking – all these are primitive wolf behaviours that have come down the generations since the start of domestication all those years ago.

Only in sleeping behaviour do we see a divergence between wolf and dog. Wolf pups begin to lie separately from other members of the litter at about six weeks old, and they continue to follow this pattern of remaining close to their fellows, but not intertwined with them, for the rest of their lives. Dog puppies always lie in a heap, drawing warmth from each other, and when they are adult, they will always choose to lie on top of, or curled around, other dogs or cats if they are available as companions. And if no dog or cat is handy, your huge Newfoundland or your little Chihuahua will sleep on your feet or as near to you as he can possibly get. This is pack behaviour expressed in domestic terms and it is behaviour in which we, the alpha members of the pack, take considerable pleasure.

LEARNING THROUGH OBSERVATION

The natural behaviour of our pet dogs is fascinating to observe, but never forget that although you feel you know a lot about your dog, he knows even more about you, because he has the opportunity and time to watch you constantly. Nearly all dogs could write an interesting and candid treatise about their owners, their manners and habits. Perhaps we should be glad that dogs have not yet been educated that far.

Many dogs spend the greater part of their day in a light sleep, always ready to alert to unfamiliar noises or strange voices and footsteps. In the evenings, when all the family is gathered together and the house is secure, the dog will fall into a much deeper sleep. Ears are still tuned to sound,

particularly to strident high-pitched brass notes. Many dogs will howl in what seems to be actual pain at some music on television – often the signature tunes of particular programmes. It is kind to turn down the sound when these painful episodes occur.

The dog has plenty of vocalisation modes of his own; many dogs will 'sing' with their owners, or they will make a low conversational sound, which is not a growl and should never be mistaken as such.

Dogs utilise a great deal of body language, both with other animals and with humans. The dog giving an alarm against intruders will 'stand tall', and the muscles along the centre back will elevate the hair in that area so as to make the dog look as large and aggressive as possible.

The dog will make as deep a bark as he is capable of, and will continue to bark, unless stopped, until the intruder has gone away. Although barking can be annoying, especially to neighbours, it can be very useful. If a dog has got shut into a room, he will bark to communicate his plight.

The tail is also a very good mood indicator. Held stiffly behind, it is part of the attack preparation; waving or wagging from side to side with ears pricked up indicates pleasure and happy anticipation. A tail held downwards and between the hind legs signals an acknowledgement of guilt or a mood of submission, especially when it is followed by the dog going into the crouch position with ears lowered. Eyes are the critical organs of facial expression. Soft brown eyes can harden dramatically and the whole face is under tension when one dog threatens another. Yet, when spoken to kindly by the owner, the eyes soften and the facial muscles relax. Some breeds, the Labrador is an example, will draw back their lips and show their teeth in a fine imitation of a smile – a very heart warming greeting from a dog that you know.

Chapter Two

PUPPY DEVELOPMENT

In the wild, wolves choose their own mates, and the mated pair will often stay together for life. Their offspring will exhibit the characteristics they inherit from their parents quite strongly.

Every wolf pack has its male pack leader, although it is not known how it is that one animal is elected to this rank. While he is young, healthy and vigorous this male will dominate the pack, seemingly making decisions about where and when to hunt, and quelling arguments and insubordination. We refer to the pack leader as the Alpha male.

There will also be an Alpha bitch, who is often even more aggressive than the male within the pack, but she is always submissive to the pack leader. Most observers of wolves have to study them in captivity, where the wolves' behaviour may be influenced by their artificial conditions, but those who have been able to observe packs of wolves in the wild have concluded that the Alpha bitch limits the production of cubs, when it is necessary, by attacking and chasing off other fertile bitches. If cubs are born, other than her own, she may even kill them to prevent them being reared. This seems to be an instinctive action in order to preserve territory and hunting opportunity suitable for the size of the pack. When food is scarce the Alpha bitch limits the number of cubs born and reared. However, when conditions are good, she and other females may help to rear cubs whose dam may have inadequate milk supply.

It is said that the Alpha dog mates only with the Alpha bitch; as this bitch is certainly, by reason of her rank, the most able hunter. She is probably in the best physical condition and is unlikely to be carrying any hereditary defects, such as heart problems or joint dysplasias. The mating of the Alpha wolves

Mating is rarely a matter of personal choice – as far as the dog is concerned. Photo: Carol Ann Johnson.

is akin to the mating of great athletes who also are clever thinkers and ruthless in their intention to make it possible for the pack to survive. Physical beauty is of no consequence to the wild animal, but it is likely that the Alpha pair will also be very pleasing because they are efficient, working animals.

The cubs of such a pair can be expected to be born with the capabilities of the parents; they will have strong limbs and hearts, they will be active early in life and they have the capacity to learn skills which they have inherited from their parents. They will be brought up within the pack and will have every chance to copy other wolves which are equally skilled at survival. Cubs which are weak in some way will die, or be killed by pack members. Wolf packs have no tolerance for individuals who cannot be of service to the pack.

DOMESTIC CANINES

In comparison with wolf packs, domestic dogs and bitches are at a serious disadvantage. Matings are entirely influenced by the breeder, who may be seeking to establish one trait, such as long ears or a symmetrically marked coat, while disregarding or being unaware of some other hereditary defects the stud dog or bitch may have. Few breeders today can afford the time and money to develop their own lines where the health and character of each dog is known and recorded; show wins are probably the most valued achievements.

It has been said, and with some truth, that a more ruthless attitude towards puppy rearing and the dogs and bitches which are bred from would be an advantage in improving the health and temperament of the dogs we have today. Both veterinary surgeons and dog breeders give the impression that they are sympathetically sentimental in rearing puppies which have a very tentative grip on life at birth. Several years later, some pet owner may be breeding from the bitch puppy which was plucked back from the brink of death by modern veterinary skill. There is no restriction on breeding from any dog or bitch. Even if a breeder puts a "not to be bred from" caveat on a dog or bitch, this only means that progeny from that animal cannot be registered at the national Kennel Club. The caveat cannot and does not prevent that bitch having litters or the dog from siring many litters. Despite the fact that we have today advanced veterinary medicine and much better nutrition for dogs, the canine race we know is in many ways inferior to the wild wolf.

A bitch is likely to have offspring by five or six different sires in the course of her breeding life, and the appearance and characters of her puppies may be widely divergent. A popular show-winning stud dog may sire many litters to different bitches in his lifetime. Even mongrel dogs and bitches rarely select their mates, beyond coupling with the dogs and bitches that are available and ready at the time, so it may be said that canine matings are less selective than those of wolves.

AT BIRTH

A litter is born after an average 63-day pregnancy. It is important that the pups feed from the bitch immediately they are born. The colostrum, which contains antibodies, is only present in the bitch's milk for a number of hours, or one or two days at most, and feeding on this enhanced milk is an important factor in protecting the pups against infection. When they are born naturally, the first-born and the strongest pups get the most colostrum, so it can be useful to know your puppy's ranking. A breeder of pedigree dogs should keep a record of birth weights and should also be able to identify individual puppies by a personal marking system, often different coloured nail varnish painted on the toe nails will distinguish similar coloured pups.

Birth is not infrequently by caesarean section, especially among the large-headed pedigree breeds. Where the pups are removed surgically, they may be affected by the anaesthetic their dam has been given, so their normal reactions to move towards the bitch and to latch on to her teats may be inhibited. Similarly, the bitch that has had all her litter by caesarean may not even recognise them as puppies, and she may refuse to stay with them or even try to kill them. If you go to see a litter that has been born by caesarean section, try to find out why this was necessary. If the reason was that one over-sized puppy was obstructing the birth canal, then the reason is understandable. However, if further enquiry reveals that this bitch line often needs to have surgical deliveries, then you may wish to think again if you have ambitions to breed from the bitch puppy you may buy.

NEWBORN STATUS

Puppies are born in a very immature state. They cannot see or hear, but they already have good scenting ability. They have no teeth, but a good sucking reflex; they can whine, but not bark. Their puppy coat may be quite different in colour and texture from that of adults in the breed; coats can change dramatically in the developmental stage. Young puppies have no means of adjusting their own body heat, so they must keep warm by lying close to the bitch and their littermates. Puppies are born with an immature brain and nervous system; if you see a newborn litter you will notice that the puppies twitch, jerk and stretch their limbs constantly. This reflex action helps to develop the nerve and muscle system. Propelling themselves around the whelping den by a modified crawl and slithering movement takes a lot of energy, so puppies that are restless because they are cold or hungry will not progress as well as those which are tended by a maternally minded bitch.

Newborn puppies cannot urinate or defecate without the stimulation of being licked on the abdomen and around the anus by the bitch, or an approximation of this service rendered by massage with moistened cotton wool (cotton) by a human attendant.

Where the dam is ill or has died during whelping, or where she is unwilling to look after her puppies, litters may be successfully hand-reared by a devoted breeder. However, the pups may be marginally less strong and their coats may never be as good as those of puppies reared by a bitch.

Toy breed puppies may weigh as little as 90 to 100 grams (3 to 3.5 ounces) at birth. Puppies of a medium-sized breed such as Boxers will weigh about 430 grams (15 ounces), and a really large breed like the Newfoundland may be 800 to 900 grams (28 to 32 ounces) when born. By the time they are a week old, most healthy pups will have doubled their birth-weight, and spend 30 per cent of their time feeding. By the time they are eight weeks old, puppies may be six to eight times heavier than when they were born.

EYESIGHT

The first landmark in puppy development is when the eyes gradually open, seven to ten days after birth. At this stage, the eyes will be pale blue in colour and the puppies will show a dislike of bright light. Dogs have a simple visual system, very different to that of man. Dogs cannot distinguish distant objects unless they are moving, and we do not really know what colours a dog can see. A person standing against a hedge only a short distance away may be invisible to a dog if the wind is carrying the person's scent away. Dogs with flat faces, like Boxers and Pugs, can judge distance well, but are not as long-sighted as breeds that have their eyes positioned one each side of a prominent nose, as the sheep-herding breeds do. These dogs turn their whole heads to see what is going on around them. Many dogs have very expressive eyes, which can harden in anger or soften with pleasure. A perceptive owner will learn to read their dog's facial expressions.

HEARING

Hearing becomes active in puppies when they are around two weeks old, and at three weeks the litter will be startled by unexpected loud noise. They will also begin to respond when the breeder speaks to them. This interaction becomes increasingly important from this stage onwards. Dogs' ears are so sensitive that there is never any need to shout at them. A

At about ten days of age, the eyes open. This is a litter of Shih Tzu puppies.   *Photo: Carol Ann Johnson.*

dog's ears have a great deal more capacity than our own. They can hear sounds on a much higher register than we can, and some very high pitched sounds appear to give them actual pain. The location of sound in open country seems more difficult for dogs to distinguish, and they may need hand signals to find a person calling them from a distance.

VOCALISATION
Puppies can mew and wail to express pain or discomfort from birth. Actual barking begins when hearing is established, and the whole litter will sometimes bark together in a simulation of the wolf-pack howl. Domestic dogs do not howl until they are almost adult.

It is evident that these three-week-old Shiba Inu puppies are now using their sense of hearing.

Photo: John Daniels.

MOVEMENT
Baby puppies begin to get to their feet, and are usually standing by three weeks after birth and walking soon after that. Active play with other members of the litter begins at three or four weeks, and when toys to stimulate activity are given, physical skills develop quite rapidly from this stage onwards. The acquisition of skills always varies between members of the litter, and some may be almost a week behind the others in the stages of development. When the puppies have control of limb and body movements, they will move away from the nest to urinate or defecate and the dam no longer needs to stimulate them to perform these functions. Both sexes use the squat position to urinate at this stage; the

males will not usually achieve the leg-raising stance until they are about a year old.

DENTITION

The first teeth can be felt erupting in the puppies' gums when they are about two or three weeks old; weaning on to solid food may begin at this time. A full set of 28 milk teeth will be in place within a few weeks, and the bitch may then be reluctant to feed her puppies. She will still give them a lot of care and an equal amount of discipline. At about four months old, the permanent teeth begin erupting in the puppy's jaw, gradually pushing out the milk teeth. The puppy should have his full set of 42 permanent teeth by the time he is six months old.

SCENT

Dogs, like wolves, have a very sophisticated sense of smell, which they utilise to mark their territory, and, we believe, also to find out who else has been there, and to detect the identities and the histories of other dogs that have passed that way. Urine marking is very important in the canine world, and so is anal sniffing of fellow canines. There is no evidence that defecation is used in the same manner.

THE VALUE OF PLAY

The puppies will at first play on their own, and then will begin to interact with their fellows in a contest to gain ownership of the toy which they find most desirable. Inevitably, toes, tails and earflaps will be squashed or bitten and squeals will result, but no actual harm is done in these

The interaction between littermates is a vital part of the learning process.

trial and error contests between puppies of the same age. It will soon be possible to identify the puppy that is always the leader, and the one that would rather stay in the quiet and safety of the den. These roles seldom alter very much once they are established, but knowing the characters of the individual puppies helps the breeder to place each one where owner and puppy will suit each other best.

LEARNING FROM THE DAM

The advice given in many quarters when considering puppy buying is to see the puppies with the mother, but this should actually be emphasised as: see the puppies *interacting* with their mother. This serves to make clear that the bitch you are being shown actually gave birth to the litter, and, even more importantly, you will find that you can learn a lot from the way the bitch behaves with the pups. For the first three weeks, the litter is entirely dependent on the bitch. You will notice that she is very solicitous for their welfare – if a pup squeals or squeaks, she will be quick to turn to see the reason why; she will comfort the pup with a lick and probably ease it up to one of her teats to feed.

From the age of three weeks onwards, the pups go into a very important stage when their attitude to people, other animals and the busy outside world is being formed. The puppy becomes aware of the other members of the litter; the puppy learns how to play, how to defend himself, how to attack, and how to behave as a member of the canine race. By the time the pups are four or five weeks old, they are becoming independent of the bitch for feeding, but she will still spend time with them, playing a little and teaching them even more.

Puppies bite the bitch's tail and paws, and she will tolerate or even encourage these actions, until either she has had enough play or the pup concerned is biting too hard. The bitch moves her paw away, but the pup goes after it. The bitch gives a low warning growl; the pup persists in the game, and the bitch snaps loudly, close to the pup's head but not actually making contact. The puppy is frightened of the reaction he has received, and after several repetitions, he will learn that biting mother's paws is not the thing to do.

This little scenario is fascinating to watch, because the bitch is educating her puppies in acceptable behaviour – and that is what you, the new owner, must do too. Never harm the puppy, never hit the puppy, but make it clear by sharp noise and

Watch the mother with her puppies, and this will give you an idea of overall temperament.

actions when some behaviour pattern is not to be tolerated. Physical punishment is not needed. A bang on the table close to the puppy is all that is necessary to startle him into awareness that you are not pleased.

Dogs learn very quickly that good behaviour can bring a reward, such as a treat or a lot of pleasurable petting, and that bad behaviour results in being ignored or reproached. Even puppies are very quick to learn the difference; they read our faces and our tone of voice and soon appreciate when they are approved of and when they are not. It is wrong to let disapproval go on for very long – remember the dam's behaviour and turn the sunshine on again soon.

The most important lesson you can learn from the bitch for use with your dog all of his life is to reprimand *quickly*, as soon as the error has been made. Dogs live by the minute; they do not look back, so grumbling or admonishing a dog for something he did ten minutes or ten hours ago is useless, and verging on cruelty. The obvious conclusion to draw from that statement is that, especially while the puppy is young, you, or someone equally responsible, must be around and keeping an eye on the puppy all the time. Apart from having the opportunity to correct the puppy when he is chewing the best chair cover, you are also in a position to stop further damage being done.

Do not allow your puppy to misbehave; make it possible for the pup to be right all the time, and this way you establish

good behaviour as a way of life. When the puppy is about to destroy something precious, distract his attention and make him focus on something you can do together, such as a short game with a tugging toy or rolling the puppy over to tickle his tummy. Let the puppy get into the habit of concentrating on the humans in the household; being around you and sharing your day and activities as much as is possible. Making a pup's life interesting keeps him out of mischief, and if the pup stays around you, you always know where he is and what he is doing and automatically, you have the advantage of keeping your puppy out of trouble.

THE IMPORTANCE OF SOCIALISATION

It is important that puppies are reared by the breeder within the house. Here, the pups have the opportunity, from their earliest days, to become familiar with the noise of household machinery such as washing machines, mixers, oven timers etc., and where they can see people passing, and be spoken to and handled frequently. Puppies that are reared in outside kennels or sheds, even if brought inside the house for short periods, will never be as confident and adaptable as puppies that have lived in the world humans inhabit. An enclosure constructed of wire panels enables the puppies to see and be seen and to become even more part of the human environment. A large box turned on its side in one corner of the play area will be needed to serve as a sleeping den. Some

A well socialised dog will take all situations in his stride.

form of entry for the bitch must also be arranged, so that she can visit the puppies, but also get away from them when she wants to.

Socialisation means accustoming puppies to as many as possible of the experiences they will meet in later life. Puppies are ready to begin experiencing the smells and sounds of the world at two weeks old, but between 7 and 14 weeks is the critical time for accustoming puppies to new experiences. Obviously, pups living in the house must be confined in a suitable area for their own safety. From now on, visitors of all ages and of both sexes should be encouraged to spend a few minutes with the puppies, and to pick them up carefully, if the bitch has no objection. Holding the puppies close to the human body helps them to become accustomed to human scent – predominantly the acid sweat odour given off by humans, but do take care when children are holding puppies as they can squeeze them too tightly. It is important that children should bond with the puppy, so ask them to sit cross-legged on the floor and to hold the puppy in their laps – then there is less chance of an accident.

Some dog breeding households lack a cross-section of human inhabitants – some pups will only have heard female voices; some will have never experienced being handled or spoken to by men; and some will have never known or heard babies, children or elderly people. All these categories of human can seem very different to young puppies and, indeed, to older dogs too, if they have grown up in adult and

predominately female households, as many dogs do.
Introducing other dogs, and cats too, is also important for
early socialisation.

Puppies of up to 12 weeks of age can respond eagerly to
people and events, but they may show acute fear to these
same occurrences if they encounter them for the first time at
six months of age. Obviously, conditioning puppies from such
a young age makes the breeder's task much more onerous
than it was when puppies were kept outside in kennels,
needing only feeding and cleaning until they were ready to be
sold. Now, it is seen as imperative that well socialised puppies
should receive a great deal of mental stimulation between the
age of two weeks and their selling age of seven to nine
weeks. The breeder needs to spend a lot more time with the
puppies, as well as devising opportunities for the pups and the
dam to encounter new situations.

Because it is almost 20 years since a widespread epidemic
of infectious canine disease occurred, there is not such an
urgent need to keep young puppies segregated. It is useful to
ask all kinds of people in to see the puppies, as every one will
be a different experience for the puppies. And you and your
family, as the prospective buyers of a puppy, should visit
really often, handle your puppy a lot, call his name, and even
leave a worn glove or a scarf in the puppy pen, to imprint
your scent on the puppy.

The puppies should also get some outdoor experience early
on, and be allowed to run on grass or play in fallen leaves, but
at first the puppies may be unhappy in bright outdoor light.
While the risk of infection is not great, they should
nevertheless not be put in any situation that may harm them,
so they should not be put down on pavements (sidewalks) or
taken to parks and open spaces that are frequented by other
dogs. But, it is a good idea to carry a little puppy on to the
street, perhaps to stand for a while on a corner while noisy
traffic goes by, or to watch a neighbour easing his car out of
the garage.

See Socialisation page 188.

Chapter Three

TAKING A DOG INTO YOUR HOME

While the puppy was with the litter, his first teacher was his mother. She supplied food, warmth, comfort and protection from danger, as well as elementary education in social behaviour with other dogs. At weaning time, the breeder takes over these roles, supplying food, keeping the puppies clean and giving reassurance whenever something new occurs in the puppy environment. The breeder's familiar voice, which the pups will have become accustomed to ever since they could hear, will alert the pups to play and feeding time and also soothe them when they settle down. The play and feeding time calls will sound subtly different to the pups, but they take the place of the hunting calls of their wolf ancestors.

When you take the puppy into your own home, you take over

When a puppy leaves its mother and its littermates, you must take on the role of teacher, comforter and playmate.

Photo: Carol Ann Johnson.

the teaching role as well as being the provider, comforter and games-captain, and so you assume the responsibility for your pup's happiness and well being. Being the educator does not imply that you only administer discipline; you and the rest of your family protect, comfort and share the good times and the jokes too, and you order your puppy's life so that it is always as enjoyable as possible. Doing what the more capable members of the pack want is a natural response in the canine world, and it is your role to make it always possible for the dog to see and understand what you want, and so to do as you wish.

You must do a lot of planning and have a lot of discussion within your household before you get to the exciting day when you bring the puppy home.

DEFINING WORDS

Now is the time to decide upon the puppy's name, although this can be altered or adapted later. Most dogs will respond to a variety of names because it is the voice-sound they hear and not the precise vocabulary. Other words and actions should be defined – what will you say when you want the puppy to urinate and/or defecate? We say "outside"; guide dogs for the blind respond to "Hurry Up". A useful piece of advice is not to make your word too domestic or babyish, as you may have to say it in public!

"No!" is going to be your most frequently used word, and it can be a life-saver. "Sooty, No!" can arrest a dog just about to jump the fence or purloin a steak. "No!" is the ultimate deterrent, and if the word is used from puppyhood, it means what it says to the end of the dog's days. *See Commands page 113, See Vocabulary page 201.*

PUPPY PERMITTED AREAS

Decide what areas of the house the puppy may use, and get every one in the family to agree to keep the puppy within that area, and not in other rooms unless someone is able to supervise him. It is always wise to fence off the stairs and not to allow puppies to climb until they are well grown. Rushing up and down the stairs may seem to be fun, but it is very bad for immature bones and muscles as well as being dangerous to dogs and to humans. If you want the puppy to go upstairs, you must carry him up and down. You will be well advised to buy a baby-gate for the stairs to stop the puppy roaming. We also have a temporary gate between the kitchen and dining area, again so that the pup can see and be seen.

Being effective about the puppy permitted areas means that members of the household must train themselves to shut doors, and they must discipline themselves to be exceptionally tidy with personal belongings. Puppies will take and attempt to destroy personal articles of clothing and bags, notebooks, diaries etc. that are left accessible. You will notice that the things the puppy takes are those that a member of the family has just handled, which very obviously carry the recent scent of the home pack. Having issued this warning, if the puppy marks or tears something a member of the family values, it is some human's fault and not the puppy's, because things that are valued should not be left within the puppy's reach. Humans can learn from this training period too.

THE INDOOR CRATE

Buy or borrow a folding wire crate. You will find it invaluable for the first year of a pup's life, because the crate can be erected anywhere, for instance in a friend's house if you are visiting, or in the garden if you want to keep the puppy safe while you are working. With the door of the crate ajar, it is the pup's bed, his little safe house where he can go when he is tired or does not want to be disturbed. The great virtue of the wire crate is that the puppy can see all that goes on around him.

The crate is exceptionally useful when you are cooking or decorating, or when guests or workmen are present. A shut out puppy is an outcast from the pack and feels lonely and miserable and probably gets up to mischief, while the pup observing everything from his wire crate is learning all the time. Get a large enough crate to hold the dog when he becomes an adult, and in the meantime pad it into a small space with bedding. You will never regret the investment. *See Crate training page 117.*

PUPPY PROOFING

Puppies explore, investigate, sample leaves and plants, taste everything, chase and catch bees, wasps and flies – a puppy's early life is one of adventure and of preparation for the primeval hunt, just as his ancestors' was. Some of the adventures and sampling may be dangerous to the pup's health, or even fatal. Since no one can provide an absolutely danger-free environment, the only alternative is to watch your puppy intensively, and check frequently on what he is doing, especially when he is in the garden.

Now, before you get your precious pup, is the time to make your boundaries secure. Look at fencing and hedging, for gaps or worn areas, and for spaces underneath. Puppies love to dig – small terriers and Dachshunds were bred for their digging ability. If you have a digging breed, boundary wire fencing is best buried about four inches below ground level.

The fastenings of gates warrant inspection. Make sure that back entrances to your property, and especially the front gate, fasten easily and securely so that callers can shut them properly and quickly and your puppy cannot escape. Then, take a critical look at the garden to find danger areas – unfenced swimming pools and garden ponds are death traps for puppies; they do not understand the difference between water and land. Swimming pools partially covered in winter are a special danger area, and cause the deaths of several dogs every year, because even adult dogs do not realise there is water underneath the cover – they appear to be solid, and this is particularly true when there is a fall of snow. Dogs drown within minutes when they cannot climb out of a straight-sided pool. Temporary fencing is prescribed around any sort of hazard. Can drain outlets be covered over? A puppy can become trapped in a drain with hot water gushing all over him. Put away all garden tools and chemicals, especially slug pellets and weed killers, even if they are said to be harmless to animals. Because slug pellets may be carried away from neighbours' gardens by birds and then dropped on your patch, it is sensible to ask neighbours if they will be kind enough to refrain from using any poisonous substances either. Slug pellets are sweet to taste and seem irresistible to pets, but even a few pellets can bring about collapse and convulsions leading to death unless you can get veterinary attention for your dog within a few minutes.

Sometimes birds, rats and mice that have been poisoned elsewhere will die in your garden. Carcasses have a natural attraction for dogs, so be sure to find them before your dog does and dispose of them safely.

Tidy up dumps of disused materials, especially old tins of paint, discarded anti-freeze, pieces of old timber which may have been painted with lead-based paint (very poisonous if chewed by a dog), and old car batteries. Old bath tubs used as water containers should be covered, and make sure the puppy cannot climb into the rainwater container. Some puppies will climb a pile of logs or a fallen tree just as easily as a kitten can.

Puppies love to explore, so make sure your garden is safe – and escape-proof.   *Photo: Keith Allison.*

Decide what would be the easiest and safest drill to follow when opening the front door to callers. Your puppy should be friendly, inquisitive and eager to greet callers, but the danger of him running out on to the road must never be forgotten. Devise a routine for door answering. Will you have the indoor kennel in the hall, ready to pop the puppy in before you open the front door, or is it easier to put him into the kitchen first? Opening the door on a safety chain does not work for puppies, as the gap between door and frame is usually large enough to let the puppy wriggle out.

Whatever you decide, all the family must follow the same drill, saying the same words. We say "this way, this way" as we hustle our dogs into the kitchen, where they wait until either the caller has left or been invited in.

Electrical connections are an attraction and a major danger. Eliminate all trailing wires and never leave an electric appliance attached to its socket where a puppy can reach. When leaving the puppy alone, in utility room or kitchen, make sure the puppy cannot get near the source of electricity.

Puppies and older dogs watch their owners constantly, even when you are unaware of it. They want to do what you do, and find the things which, to you, are just cans and packets, interesting and exciting. Make sure that all the kitchen cupboards have effective puppy-proof fastenings, and do close them properly after use. The cupboard where cleaning fluids and soaps are kept is the most dangerous. Soap has an attraction for puppies that can prove fatal. A tablet of soap taken into the mouth will create large quantities of foam mixed with saliva, which will choke a dog very quickly. Make sure all soap is well out of canine reach.

See Containment page 114.

TOYS

Acquire a few canine toys before your pup moves in; make sure they are quality objects that will not easily be destroyed. Fragments of plastic and rubber and the squeakers out of toys are dangerous if swallowed. Some breeds simply love squeaky toys and get very excited, sometimes even over-excited, as they try to 'kill' the squeak, just as their ancestors killed small prey. A soft toy, such as a small teddy bear, will give a lot of pleasure, and so will a piece of thick rope for tug of war games with humans.

See Games page 138.

Toys must be safe and durable.
Photo: Carol Ann Johnson.

COLLAR AND LEAD

Buy a soft, lightweight collar for your puppy. This can be replaced with a stronger, leather collar when your puppy is about three months old. A lead will also be needed. There are a variety of collars and leads available, and some are particularly suitable for coping with training problems.
See Collars page 111, Leads, Leash and Lead Training page 157.

IDENTIFICATION

Before your puppy comes home, arrange to have a nametag engraved with your name and address and/or telephone number. Nametags can be obtained at pet stores or from some of the animal charities.

More permanent identity marking may be achieved by an electronic chip painlessly implanted by a veterinary surgeon under the skin at the back of the neck. The chip, with its individual number which gives the owner's identity, can be decoded by a reading device which most veterinary surgeries will own. Tattooing an individual registered number in the ear or on the abdomen is also an option, but this will have to wait until the puppy has grown on a little more. Both identity chip and tattooed identities are registered with appropriate authorities so that the dog may easily be returned to the owners if it strays or is stolen.
See Straying page 193.

CLEANING UP

One of the less pleasant aspects of dog ownership is cleaning up after your dog. If your dog fouls in a public place, it is your duty to clean up after him. This is easily accomplished with a 'scoop', or just by using a plastic bag. In most places, there are bins where you can dispose of waste. Go to your local pet store, and equip yourself, so you are prepared right from the start.
See House training (outside the home) page 152.

GIVING CONFIDENCE

One of your main tasks in the early days of puppy ownership is to give your puppy confidence in your family and in other people. Puppies are most impressionable between the ages of 8 and 12 weeks, and all their early experiences must be happy ones. You will obviously need to deter the puppy from doing things that are harmful to him and to your furnishings, but do

Puppies are at their most impressionable between 8-12 weeks, so learning experiences should be positive and pleasurable.

it in a positive and happy way. Distract the puppy with a food treat or another toy. Always call the puppy to you in a happy voice; get down to puppy level and open your arms wide to welcome him when he comes to you and then make a big fuss of him. Make coming when called worthwhile, always. Puppies learn very easily how to receive and give pleasure.

As dog owners, it is our job to convey in every way we can that we are the source of food, warmth, approval, games, fun and everything that is good in a dog's life. Dogs genuinely want to please their owners; during puppy days you have to show how pleased you are with the pup by physical petting. Later in life, the dog will only need your smile and comfortable expression to know that he is what he wants to be – "the best dog in the world".

OLDER DOGS

When they hear how much a puppy has to be taught, and what a lot of time must be devoted to puppy education, many people feel it would be easier to acquire an older dog. Certainly, there are many deserving dogs looking for second or third homes, but there is no guarantee that adopting them will be easy. Taking on a dog that has lost his previous home is a very worthy thing to do, but to create a special relationship with such a dog may be far from easy. Some dogs may show tangible gratitude and joy at becoming part of your family, and may seem to soon forget that they ever belonged to anyone else, but experiences early in life make an indelible impression on the canine mind, and are sometimes never eradicated.

If you are fortunate enough to know the dog's previous owners personally, and you are aware that they have some irrefutable reason for it being necessary to part with their pet, then you have a number of advantages. You should be able to get a true picture of the dog's history and you will be able to learn his language and the commands his previous owners used.

Be sure to make in-depth enquiries about any misdemeanours the dog may have committed so that you can guard against similar situations occurring. It may be that your lifestyle is quite different, and so you are able to prevent sins, such as constant barking or destruction when left alone. It is true that some owners do feel conscience pangs about not being able to cope with the dog which they once wanted so much, and they may not be entirely frank about any faults in their dog's character.

Dogs that have shown themselves to be aggressive with children are probably always going to be a risk, even if you have no immediate young family of your own. Always get a veterinary report on the adult dog you propose to acquire, so that you are aware of any tendency to illness. Any information you can get will help you to get on good terms with the dog.

You will probably have knowledge of the previous owner's physical stature and that of members of the family, so you will have some idea of what memories may be awakened in the dog if similar people are encountered in your home. While scent is an important recognition factor to the dog, the outline of a familiar person, their walk and their voice, may also convey a lot. Sympathetic treatment of your new pet is indicated, but always keep the mood jolly, he is not a 'poor dog', but a lucky dog to have been chosen again.

RESCUED DOGS
Giving a home to a dog from a rescue kennel inspires a generous feeling in all of us, but such a dog may be even more difficult to educate to civilised behaviour than a puppy. In addition, the possibility is always there that the rescued

dog may be dangerous to some people in some circumstances.

The kennel staff may assure you that 'Patch' is absolutely sweet, but bear in mind that they are experienced handlers and they are caring for the dog in a protected situation. Probably no-one knows the dog's history with any accuracy; there may have been cruelty, indifference, neglect or anything else in this dog's story. It will take a long time for the dog to tell you, but he probably will eventually, because you will piece together what caused his fears and resentments from his reactions to events, situations and people he encounters while with you.

Oddly enough, many rescued dogs do not show their true character for weeks or months after they have been taken into a caring home. We go too far if we suggest that dogs are

If you give a home to an older dog, such as a retired Greyhound, you will need extra patience to gain the dog's confidence and establish a relationship.

Photo: Steve Nash.

capable of deliberate deception, but it is true that all can be sweetness and light initially in the new home. If the dog has been in kennels for some time, you will have to house-train him in just the same way as you would do a puppy. You may find territory marking is intensified in a dog that has had a life of wandering freely. The urge to jump fences and escape is strong in the rescued dog, and you may find him more inclined to fight other dogs or to chase cats. He may be more possessive of the comfort you are providing. Be very careful of your rescued dog when he is around children – never leave him unsupervised to join in their games, as you just do not know what has happened to him in a previous life. Often, some innocent action, such as raising an umbrella or handling gardening tools, or even raised voices or dropping a cake tin, may trigger an unexpected reaction in a dog that has had a bad time in the past.

EX-SHOW OR BREEDING DOGS

Sometimes dog breeders and exhibitors will have dogs that they wish to place in private homes when the dog's show career or breeding life is over. Get a veterinary check on such an offer, as the dog may have been eliminated from a breeding kennel because he has some hereditary fault which you will want to know about, even if you do not need to reject the dog for this reason.

Many kennel dogs are tremendously grateful to become an only pet, enjoying all the household comforts and human affection. But bear in mind that the dog that has been kennelled may never have been house-trained, and has almost certainly been used to the constant company of other dogs, and may not be so attuned to humans.

None of this is written to deter you from taking on a 'second-hand' dog if that is your inclination. but it does serve to warn you that there are still likely to be problems when taking a previously owned dog into your family, although they will be different problems from those you will encounter when bringing up a puppy.

Chapter Four

THE RIGHT
START

Collecting your puppy from the breeder and bringing him home is the first great pleasure in your life together, so it makes sense to do everything possible to make this journey go smoothly.

THE RIDE HOME

If you are obliged to use public transport, borrow a puppy carrier from your vet, because puppies can become uncomfortable and frightened if carried in your arms for a long time. If you are collecting by car, take a tolerant and suitably clad companion with you, so that, while you drive, he

The big day arrives when it is time to collect your puppy.

Photo: Carol Ann Johnson.

or she can reassure and restrain the puppy. The noise of the road and the sight of other traffic rushing past is almost certainly unfamiliar to the puppy, and it may be frightening, or just interesting, according to the pup's temperament. The puppy will almost certainly drool, and probably vomit. Mop up but do not otherwise worry; he will grow out of this phase in time without any need for medication or tranquillisers.

Even if being in the car frightens the puppy, do not sympathise. Talk to him, by all means, but keep your voices bright and encouraging; travel is all part of a modern dog's life, and life is going to be good for this pup!

Unless the journey is a very long one, try not to feed the puppy before the journey, but do ask the breeder to prepare a packed meal, or even two meals, so that you can see the consistency and the amount of food to be given. Give small amounts of water (not milk) to drink if needed. Unless the puppy has been fully vaccinated against infectious viral diseases, do not put him down in any place where other dogs are likely to have been.

SETTLING IN

When you arrive at your home, there will doubtless be other people waiting to greet and play with your puppy. Put him down in the garden for a few minutes, and then call him to you in a happy voice: his great life has begun! Then take the pup indoors to eat his meal. It will be useful if you have set up his crate in the kitchen already. Put the puppy inside to eat, putting the food into a small, shallow dish, and shutting the door of the crate for a few minutes. Be ready to remove the puppy at once when he has finished eating; wipe and dry his face so that food residue does not collect on his whiskers. Show him where his water dish is, then put him outside again and play with him for a few minutes – the cardboard centre from a paper towel roll makes a handy toy at this time. He should then be ready to go into his crate for a long sleep, followed by more play, more introductions, more food and another long sleep.

Whether you shut the door of the crate or not depends upon you. At this stage, it is probably better to allow the puppy a way out, if he wants one, but always keep an eye on your new pet so that you always know what he is doing – or, better still, what he is about to do. Always try to prevent your puppy doing anything that will be regarded as a misdemeanour, either now or when he is older. Distract the puppy away from

Give your puppy a chance to explore when he first arrives home. *Photo: Carol Ann Johnson.*

the forbidden object with a toy or a little physical play. Yes, bringing up a puppy is almost a full-time occupation, but you are rewarded in the end by a companion animal of which you can be proud while he is still young.

THE FIRST NIGHT

Probably the first crisis in your young puppy's life will come at the end of the first day in your home. The puppy will be tired and happy and almost overwhelmed by all the new experiences, but what if you put him into his bed, pat him and shut the room door upon him, leaving him alone in a big unfamiliar space for the first time in his life? From the pup's point of view, he is completely lost and alone.

A heated pad put under his bedding may help to soothe him initially, but the ticking alarm clock you may be advised to put in his bed is nothing like his dam's heartbeat, which it is supposed to resemble. When the puppy wakes after an hour or two of sleep, he will be acutely lonely, and frightened, too. He will probably feel a little bit cold and a little bit strange, but most of all, he will feel lonely. Litters of puppies often have a short playtime in the middle of the night – they do not habitually sleep right through for eight hours.

When your puppy wakes and is unable to find his littermates, he calls the pack to him, and what happens? Instead of playful puppies, he gets a very cross human who resents being woken and called downstairs; a human that is a little short on the patience and tolerance you have shown the puppy all day. You are in fact failing your puppy from the outset, and spoiling the bonding that has already begun, because your puppy has every right to feel lonely on his first night away from his littermates; by deserting him you have begun to spoil his trust in you. So plan ahead to minimise the first night trauma. Essentially, the puppy needs to know that he is not alone, and there are basically only two solutions.

The first is to arrange the puppy's bed beside your own in your bedroom, so that you are aroused directly the puppy stirs and can put a comforting hand out to soothe him. If you have bought a folding crate, as advised, it is simple enough to carry it upstairs to make the puppy's bed beside yours, bringing the crate down again in the morning for use downstairs during the day. A deep cardboard box that the puppy cannot climb out of will also make an improvised upstairs bed.

The second solution is to arrange a temporary bed for yourself in the kitchen or utility room where you hope the dog will sleep in future, when he has gained complete security and trust in you and familiarity with the house.

Puppies need the reassurance of a mothering presence, especially during the night; a hand put into his bed, a little stroking, a few soothing words, and your pup is off to sleep again. If he is alone in a room and has to cry and scream, frightened and bewildered, before getting attention, the puppy is a lot more difficult to settle again, and may never recover from the initial shock of being alone. He may always lack confidence and you may always have trouble getting him to stay alone even as an adult. Having the puppy close at hand also means that you can continue with house-training, taking the puppy outside directly he stirs in the early mornings.

So, no matter what your principles are about dogs in bedrooms, it is worthwhile tolerating a puppy close to you for a week or two until he has learnt a lot more about your house and his new family. There is no need for a puppy or an older dog ever to sleep in or on the human bed, but the box at the bedside is convenient and comforting.

You may deduce that someone is in for some disturbed nights in the early days of puppy ownership, and that is inevitably so because we have to accustom a little animal to conform to the shape of our own days. Puppies cannot learn to live in a human environment unless they are taught to do so by humans.

Canine learning has to be constant and continuous, and always done in the same way, using the same words and the same hand signals. Within a few weeks, when you feel the pup has complete confidence in you and is familiar with your

*The new puppy may feel almost overwhelmed
by the end of the first day.*

home, and has also spent some time alone during the day, you
will be able to try leaving him alone at night, if that is what
you intend to do. However, companion dogs often do spend
their nights in the same room as a member of their human
family, because this emphasises the dog and human roles as
protector and caretaker.

HOUSE-TRAINING

This is the first, and most important, lesson to teach your
puppy in order that he becomes a socially acceptable member
of the family. It is important to establish a routine, and to be
as vigilant as possible.
See House training page 149.

ADULT DOGS: Except in times of illness or extreme
agitation, adult dogs have extremely good bowel and bladder
control. They will go out when you invite them to do so.
Healthy adults may only need to defecate twice a day and to
pass urine perhaps three or four times. Illness, such as cystitis,
will lead to increased urination, and any digestive upset will
provoke increased frequency of defecation.

Elimination control will inevitably relax during illness or
when some unwise eating has caused loose bowel
movements. The quality, colour and frequency of passing
faeces is a very important indication of a fault in the digestive

system of the dog, so it is always useful to be aware what your dog is passing. Then, you can report accurately to the vet if the changed state goes on for more than a day or two.

Sometimes a dog will adopt a mute protest more common to the cat family, and will begin to soil indoors because something is causing the dog mental stress, jealousy or aggravation. The culprit may be a new pet taking attention, a new baby, or even someone new in the household who is, for some reason, incompatible with the dog. Only you can determine the problem and devise a solution acceptable to all.

Male dogs, especially, will pass small quantities of urine when out for a walk. This is deliberate urine marking to establish his own identity and status in the neighbourhood rather than a need to empty the urinary bladder. A male dog may find the need to re-mark his home territory if he has been away for some time, or if other animals (cats or foxes) have passed that way overnight. You will often find that a male dog will choose a particular shrub for his marking post. Male dog urine directed at a plant will almost certainly kill the vegetation, and it can be the wisest course to leave the dead plant in situ, rather than replacing it with another, which will meet the same fate. Adult bitch urine kills grass and spoils lawns. The only remedy is to pour on a couple of buckets of water directly the urine has been deposited, and then to re-train the bitch to use concrete or a patch of earth left vacant for the purpose.

Many households will arrange to have a suitable exit made in a back door, possibly leading to a small enclosed yard, so that the dog can get out to relieve itself during the night or while no one is home.

FEEDING

Eight-week-old puppies are usually fed four times a day at fixed times which will suit your household. Try to keep to the appointed mealtime as accurately as you can. At twelve weeks, the pup will require more food as he grows and his activity increases, but at this age food is usually divided into three meals, usually given at room temperature, in the early morning, middle of the day and early evening. If you are giving small treats to encourage behaviour training, make these very small or deduct them from the daily food allowance, because overfeeding a young puppy can be a disaster with regard to excess development of bone and muscle, which may cause orthopaedic problems later on.

Top-quality food, served at regular times, is a must for growing puppies.   *Photo: Carol Ann Johnson.*

Dogs are attracted to food more by smell than by taste. A reluctant feeder may respond to the food being slightly warmed, or by the addition of something with a strong smell, such as sardines or a small amount of a pungent canned cat food. Do not be tempted to give cat food as the entire meal, as it is constituted very differently from dog food and does not suit dogs in the long term. Beware that dogs are great habit formers and can be very despotic about their wants. If a dog realises that if he hesitates over his food dish, something more exciting will be added to it, you will soon find that he will not eat at all without the additional flavouring.

If a puppy refuses food that he has previously eaten eagerly, try to find out why. Is the food you are offering too hot or too cold? Is another dog or a cat threatening the puppy so that he is afraid to eat? Is there an unfamiliar person watching the pup, or are there unusual noises in the house? Are you usually in the habit of watching the puppy while he eats, but have you found something more urgent to do this time? In many ways, it is a good idea to watch the puppy while he eats, but you could also be training him to demand your presence, or he refuses to eat his meal.

Offer the food to a reluctant eater for five minutes and then take it away, covering the dish against flies. Some 15 minutes later, try the puppy with the food again. If you still get a refusal, take the puppy outside to relieve himself and watch what he does; he may have some digestive upset, or he may have swallowed a toy that is causing problems coming through the system. One of my puppy bitches passed a whole facecloth, as good as new except that all the colour was bleached out, and another day she voided a toy rubber mouse. Not everyone is so lucky – vets are constantly operating on dogs that have their intestines entirely obstructed by all manner of different things – a pair of socks, an audio tape or even a plastic doll.

If a puppy continues to refuse food for several hours, see if he will drink, preferably boiled water and glucose. It would be wise at this stage to inform your vet, in case it is necessary to see the puppy at once, or they may want you to report in a certain number of hours if the situation has not altered. Young puppies can become dangerously dehydrated very quickly, and may need to be given fluid through an intravenous drip. In any case, your puppy will probably require expert diagnosis and help to find the reason for the refusal of food and drink.

It is important to keep the puppy on the exact food on which he was reared for several weeks after he comes into your home. Then, if you want to alter the diet, add the new element in small quantities, gradually increasing the amount until you are feeding a complete meal of the food of your choice. Observe the internal reaction of the puppy to the food that you have chosen; if there are loose, liquid faeces or a lot of gas in the stomach, then that food does not suit your puppy. In any case, it is wise to weigh the puppy to check that his weight gain is gradual and even. Your vet probably has electronic scales on which you can weigh the puppy without needing to pay for a consultation. In any case, standing still upon the scales for a few seconds is good disciplinary training.

There are a lot of very effective and nutritious commercially prepared foods in dried or canned formulation on the market now, obtainable at supermarkets, specialist pet shops and also delivered directly to your home. It makes good sense to use one of these complete foods for your puppy. Home-cooked meals can be difficult to provide and to store properly, and you will find that the commercially devised foods give full instructions about feeding at different ages.

Dogs do not require variety in their diet. The balanced menu that your puppy enjoys and thrives on can be provided

Variety in the diet is not essential for dogs.
Photo: Steph Holbrook.

every day for most of your dog's life, and he will be all the better for having consistency in his diet. In illness and old age, there is justification for modifying or adjusting the food to suit the condition of the dog, but even then there are scientifically prepared diets which will supply the right balance of protein, fat and carbohydrate to suit a dog with a specific illness.

Otherwise, for the healthy dog, one good-quality dried diet, with possibly the addition of a few household scraps of meat, fish or cheese, will suit your dog very well, every day of the year, although you must upgrade to the different age formulas the manufacturer provides as your puppy grows. Clean, fresh water must always be available for the dog, inside and outside the house. Take care that water left outside is not contaminated by birds or other animals.

STEALING: Puppies and dogs do not steal food – they just take food which careless humans have left within their reach. Realise what your puppy is likely to do and guard against anything edible or otherwise attractive being left where the dog can reach it. Dogs have been known to snatch frozen food straight out of the freezer, roasted joints straight out of the oven and sausages straight off the barbecue. This is not the dog's fault – the canine race is predominantly opportunist, still grabbing the prey which is easiest to obtain.

POSSESSIVENESS: When your puppy is feeding well, try removing the dish for a moment or two while he is eating, and then returning the dish, possibly with the addition of an extra treat. The puppy has to realise that you, the provider of all food, also have the right to take the food away. Most puppies quickly realise that they come very low in the feeding hierarchy and are willing, if reluctant, to let their food be taken away. The puppy that growls in these circumstances could be heading for trouble over a highly developed and exaggerated possessive instinct.

Growl sternly at the puppy when he growls at a human, but then give the food back and praise the pup. Try taking the food away again in a few minutes and see what the reaction is then. This discipline will have to be practised until the puppy understands that giving up the food without protest brings praise and affection from his owner. The possession of food is a primitive canine instinct that is nearer the surface in some breeds than in others. It is never wise to let children, cats or other dogs interfere with a dog while he is eating.

Most dogs, when they realise that they always get fed regularly, cease to feel an urgent necessity to guard food and are willing to have their bowl removed, especially if it is usually more delicious than when it went away. Always remove feeding bowls when the meal is finished, as some adult dogs will get possessive about the bowl itself. Water does not inspire the same feelings, so a water bowl should always be available.

SNATCHING: Some dogs, often those of the larger breeds, take food rewards from our hands very softly. But other breeds are more inclined to snatch. This can be troublesome especially where children are concerned. Raising a warning finger to the dog, say "Gently, gently", removing the treat from the dog's reach if a snatch is attempted.

GROOMING
When you have had your puppy for a few days, begin daily grooming sessions to accustom him to being handled in a way which is more purposeful than petting. Smooth-coated dogs are not likely to need grooming every day, but long-coated

A daily grooming will accustom your puppy to being handled.

Photo: Amanda Bulbeck.

ones will, and you will be glad that you have taught your puppy to submit to the routine, because it makes no sense at all to have a daily tussle just to keep him looking smart.

Place the puppy on a steady table, or on your lap – whichever suits you best. Your breeder should have shown you the type of grooming tools, especially the brushes and comb, which suits your breed best. Canine grooming tools come in a large range and are not inexpensive, so it is wise to invest in the correct kit from the start.

Show the puppy the brush and comb you propose to use, and perhaps play with them a little, so that the puppy sees that there is nothing to be afraid of. Then, start to comb gently. You will probably find that the puppy sheds a lot of his fluffy baby coat; this has to go before the adult coat comes through. The puppy may also be changing coat colour for the adult shade. Five minutes' grooming time is ample, and there should be a reward to come when the time is up. On another day, you can concentrate on checking the ears for dirty wax, and looking at the teeth to check that no adult teeth are coming through before the baby teeth are shed (which starts when the pup is about four months old). Get the veterinary nurse at your practice to show you the ear-cleaning routine and sell you the right preparations. Never, ever use a cotton bud on a dog's ears.

You may have to pay a little attention to the dog's rear end, and to the penis of the male, as long hair in this area can get soiled and puppies do not generally attempt to clean themselves.

Always make the conclusion of a grooming session your decision. The puppy must submit until you have finished, but never get angry if he struggles – just be firm and determined. There is no weaker admission of failure than to have to say "he won't let me", and there is no more of a shaming spectacle than a long-haired dog that is dirty, tangled and unkempt because the owner cannot groom him.

When you have finished the daily grooming session, put the equipment away in a drawer. The fact that you began by playing with the puppy with these tools to get him used to them may lead to the pup treating the grooming set as a toy, and that is not what is wanted at all.

See Grooming acceptance pages 142.

BATHING

It may not be really necessary to bath your puppy, but it is another experience he must learn to tolerate. Small puppies can be bathed in a sink or a washbowl, or in a larger container on the kitchen floor.

Use a shampoo made for dogs, not one for humans, as dog hair has a different chemical construction. When the puppy is rinsed and towel-dried, get out the hairdryer, sit with the pup on your lap, and dry gently on a mild setting, combing the hair as you work. The sooner this process is tolerated the better; the pup must learn that the hairdryer is nothing to be afraid of when you are holding him.

Adult dogs do not need regular bathing as the process will destroy the natural oils in the coat. However, there may be times when this is necessary, such as when your dog has rolled, or when he has just become too muddy or dirty to be acceptable.

A tiled shower cubicle is the easiest place for bathing, or with a large breed, it may be preferable to go outside and use a hose.

EXAMINATION

Every day, spend just a few moments encouraging the puppy to stand on a firm table for a mock veterinary examination. Turn back the ears and look into them (do not probe), tip the head towards you and look into the eyes, open the mouth and run a clean finger over the teeth. Lift the tail and make a little inspection of anal and genital areas. Lie the puppy down on his side and then roll him on his back to examine the abdomen. Then, when it is all over, give a happy treat! This little exercise teaches your puppy a reasonable amount of submission and also gives you the opportunity to notice if there are any abrasions of the skin or ticks adhering to the limbs or head, or maybe to see the black dust of flea excreta.

NAIL CUTTING

Puppies' nails grow quickly into a curve, which makes for uncomfortable walking and, eventually, to a poor gait and deformed feet. While he is really young, your puppy is probably not doing enough walking on rough ground to wear the nails down naturally although if you have access to a sandy beach a short run on the sand can help the nails a lot.

Buy from your pet shop some purpose-designed animal nail clippers; your vet or a groomer should show you how they are used. Cutting a dog's nails is often a two-person-job – one to hold the dog and to extend the leg being dealt with, and the other (possibly the most dextrous one) to actually cut the nails. No dog enjoys the process, but a little firmness and determination on your part gets the session over quite quickly, and it is another lesson learned.

Eventually it should be possible to cut your dog's nails without assistance.

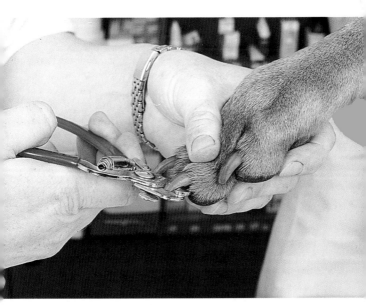

Take care not to cut into the quick of the nail.
Photo: Keith Allison.

COATS

Young, healthy dogs of the medium to large breeds rarely
need coats, unless they live in a draughty country house,
where the more elderly dog appreciates a whole-body coat.
Salukis, Whippets, Greyhounds and similar breeds with little
body fat usually wear coats outdoors in winter, especially if
they are walking slowly and perhaps having to wait around.
Coats for all breeds should cover the body and chest, and not
just protect the centre back.

HANDLING

Your puppy has to continue to tolerate handling by people
outside your own family. If you acquired your puppy with a
view to having a personal guard, do not worry that he is too
friendly with unfamiliar people. You will find that if ever it
should be necessary, your cuddly pet will respond in just the
way you hope he will – showing a formidable defence
instinct, but not being violent. Every dog's natural instinct is
to defend his home and his family members, and this trait
comes into action when it is needed. Dogs have an uncanny
instinct for recognising people who have bad intentions.

It is unwise to encourage any dog to show aggression all the
time, so let your puppy make friends with everyone who
wants to make friends with him.

TAKING MEDICINES

Inevitably, at some time in your dog's life, he will need oral
medication in the form of a tablet put down his throat, so this
is also something your puppy has to learn to tolerate.
Probably the best way of giving pills is by a little human
deception; we find the best way is to roll the capsule or tablet
in a small amount of mashed potato and offer it as if it is a
great treat. The principle is the dog will take a small ball of
mashed potato and swallow it without chewing it up and
discovering the tablet. This is certainly a better and easier
way than having to struggle to get the tablet into the throat
and having it brought up time after time. Practise giving
medication with half a vitamin tablet or a tiny piece of biscuit
wrapped in potato. It is quite amazing how dogs can secrete a
tablet within their mouths and deposit it on the carpet ages
after you think it has been swallowed.

Quite a lot of canine medication is now designed to be
palatable, so worming doses, for instance, can be given with
food. Liquid medication can be inserted in the side of the

mouth by way of an eyedropper or a hypodermic syringe (without the needle in place). Practise this technique using a spoonful of gravy. You need to cultivate this skill in case the dog is ever really ill, as you do not want to have to fight him at that time to give any prescribed medication.

THE VALUE OF PLAY

The games we play with dogs are inevitably developed from the natural behaviours of primitive dogs. These include the chasing, killing and carrying back of the prey to the den, stalking prey, jumping obstacles, scent detection, recognition of friends, finding lost objects, and physical attention such as stroking, rolling over, patting the paws, scratching behind the ears, and all manner of other interactive movements which wild animals make with each other.

Play is part of the wild canine traditional training for hunting and killing their prey. It seems that sometimes a toy, particularly one with a squeaker inside, is mistaken for live prey, and the puppy swallows the toy whole in order to keep it from being taken by a larger predatory animal. Check the toys your puppy uses.

Some breeds like to have a box of toys available to them, and the pup will choose, seemingly with great care, the toy he wants you to play with today, and the opportunity to do this helps to develop the dog's intelligence and also to bond with a human playmate. There is nothing more endearing than to see the puppy sorting over his toys and then to have a favourite one brought to you, often with major effort on the pup's part, to induce you to a mutual game. Always try to respond, however busy or tired you are – play between dog and human is a restorative therapy.

It is worthwhile mentioning that play between dog and human need not be physically exhausting. A tired person, a wheelchair-bound person or someone with physical disabilities can still create a game that satisfies both parties. Hunt-the-concealed object, throw and retrieve and deliver the object properly to have it thrown again, tug-of war, or even tickle-your-tummy games are all within the capacity of a seated human, and they can bring a lot of pleasure to both dog and human.

More active games are a joy too, for those who want to set up tracking activities, or even mini-agility courses with little tunnels and low jumps in the garden. Whatever games you play, always work towards the dog doing his part correctly so that the object of the game is fulfilled; for instance, retrieving the toy and delivering it gently so that it can be thrown again. Controlled play with humans has to be taught, just like any other dog/human interaction; dogs can become very excited about games and it may at times be necessary to cool down the interaction. Snatching or biting at hands or ankles must always mean that the game is ended abruptly, the toy taken away and the dog ignored for an hour or so until he comes up quietly again asking to play.

Adults must always remember that even though they may enjoy a physical tussle with a large dog, children and people unfamiliar with the dog may become extremely frightened. Always try to control screaming and shouting when playing with a dog; this only serves to excite the dog more and to make him even more hyperactive.

Unfortunately, there are many adults and children whose understanding of play with dogs amounts only to teasing. The dog that has been taught to play fairly does not understand

Play forms an essential part of your puppy's education, but make sure you remain in full control as the dog gets bigger.

Photo: Amanda Bulbeck.

teasing, and may be more forceful than he meant to be. Because you must protect your dog from any allegation of dangerous behaviour, you must always supervise play when new people are present. Remember that a dog's mouth and teeth are equivalent to our own facial features combined with our hands. The dog holds and carries objects with his jaws. If there is a struggle, playful or otherwise, for an object that the dog is carrying, the dog's teeth may come into contact with the human hand, inflicting a minor bite or scratch with no intention of malice behind it, but which can be turned into extremely bad news. Teach your dog to 'drop' his trophy, or at least to exchange it for food or another toy. Never try to forcibly extract an object from the dog's mouth unless the risk has to be taken, for example if the dog has grabbed something dangerous which must be removed without delay. This should only be attempted by an adult.

If a dog is played with gently from his youngest puppyhood, this will always be a rewarding part of the puppy's education and will form a basis for teaching other behaviour skills.

See Games page 138.

CHOOSING TOYS

Make sure the toys you buy are designed for dogs and not for the amusement of people. Toys made in the image of politicians or Christmas trees mean nothing to the dog. Look for toys that are shaped so that they can easily be carried by a dog, and buy good quality toys which stand up to rough treatment. A cheap plastic toy that disintegrates quickly can be a danger if the pieces are swallowed.

Random bounce toys add an extra sparkle to the throw and chase games; lengths of thick rope for tugging games are favourites. Strong, sturdy squeaker toys, which can be killed over and over again, give a lot of pleasure and are even used in the training of Search and Rescue dogs, but keep an eye on the squeak if it is likely to come out. If the toy is punctured, you must remove it with great stealth and dispose of it where it cannot be found by the dog. Puppies like soft furry toys, with and without squeaks, and large pieces of cotton rag, such as cuttings from old towels, to run about with. Nylon tights and socks are not suitable as toys. Dogs that become unduly excited when their owner returns after an absence need a stress reliever given straight away. Putting an old glove, a shoe or a conventional toy into the dog's mouth seems to

Above: Toys with a random bounce are always a favourite.
Photo: Steph Holbrook

relieve the dog's emotions in a magical way. You may want to keep an object of this kind, bearing your own scent, handy for just this greeting purpose.

It has been a convention that puppies should not be given old shoes or objects of clothing to play with, as then they will take good new objects and ruin them too. But this does not happen in your house! You will have resolved, from the earliest days of having your puppy, not to leave precious objects where the puppy can get them; nor do you allow dogs to be unsupervised in bedrooms or dressing rooms where good clothing may be left. Prevention has always, always, been far better and easier than cure. So much fun can be had from an old shoe or a discarded purse that it is a pity to dispose of such objects. Always give regular checks to such toys to make sure they are not disintegrating in such a way that they can harm the dog.

BONES
It is not advisable to give dogs meaty bones – too often, they splinter and cause problems, and a real bone seems to bring out a strong possessive instinct which it is unwise to foster. Especially made hard chewing toys are safer and cleaner to handle, they satisfy the need to chew and seem to be used by

one of my dogs to take the edge off hunger when a meal is nearly due. These bones are well worth buying as they provide activity and pleasure for months, or even years.

Another popular and easily obtainable toy is a tugger, a thick bundle of cotton threads that will take a lot of rough treatment and come out of the washing machine almost as good as new.

Balls are not such favourites with dogs as you might think. Do be extremely careful about the size of the ball you give your dog to play with; the ball must be too large for him to swallow. Puppies and dogs have choked on balls which have been caught and gone to the back of the throat in such a way that the dog cannot release the ball and the vast quantities of saliva produced makes it difficult to remove the ball from the dog's mouth. If this happens, the best first aid remedy is to grasp the dog's head on either side of his ears and attempt to push the ball forward from the outside. Never give a dog golf balls – they are too small for any size of dog; they do get swallowed but usually end up in the stomach and do not cause choking as a larger ball will. If you do buy a ball for your puppy, make sure to replace it with a larger size as he grows, but a rectangular shaped bouncing toy is much safer for him.

DOGS AND CHILDREN

Dogs and children have a special affinity. For a lonely child, a dog can be a playmate and someone to confide in; but the dog may also act as a scapegoat for the child's misdeeds. An over-disciplined child may also enjoy passing on the commands and the slaps to some creature even lower in ranking within the family, and what is more, a creature that cannot deny that he was the thief who stole the bag of sweets.

Many breeders will not sell a puppy where there is a young child of two to four years old in the family. A child of this age makes uncertain grabbing movements, which are too rough for the puppy, and the child may barely distinguish between a puppy and a stuffed teddy bear. Young children have been known to put tight rubber bands around a puppy's neck or to stuff buttons and similar objects down their ears. The puppy may become overexcited and be too rough with the child, and it really is more than one person's work to supervise the two.

Dogs that are already in the family are seldom jealous of a newborn baby, although some relatives may fear that this could happen. The behaviour training here is to show the dog

Dogs and children have a natural affinity, but both must learn a mutual respect.   Photo: Keith Allison.

the baby as soon as he or she is brought into the house and allow the dog to sniff the baby to get the scent. Let the dog be present, and perhaps be rewarded, for quiet behaviour when the baby is fed or its toilet attended to. Most importantly, the dog should still be talked to and involved in all the family activities, as well as being given just as much affection as before.

It has to be acknowledged that a puppy or growing dog can be too rough with a young child, so never leave the two unsupervised and do not let the dog be around when other children come in to play. Sometimes, dogs can be very possessive about family toys and may resent an unfamiliar child handling them. Dogs do sometimes make mistakes about other people's intentions, so it is necessary to keep watch when visitors are present.
See Children page 107.

STRANGERS
Children and adults should be warned not to loom over a dog,

standing close to him and extending a hand over his head. This is a threatening attitude from the dog's level, and may provoke an unwelcome reaction. If the dog seems a little wary of a visitor, ask him or her to take no notice of the dog, and particularly not to make eye contact. To a hostile dog, eye contact can be a challenge, although nervous people will sometimes feel compelled to watch the dog constantly, as if waiting for him to attack, with fear their dominating emotion. If there is any aggression felt between the dog and the visitor, eye contact will fan that flame. This is the time to put the dog in his crate, where he can study the visitor and vice versa in perfect safety.

Sometimes, perfectly friendly dogs will show dislike of perfectly friendly people, and we may never know why. It may be something in the human's scent, or some old memory of cruelty by a person of similar shape or smell or voice being brought to the surface. Or, there may be some contact there of which you know nothing. We had an employee who appeared to be very good with the dogs, although they had a strong dislike of him. We eventually found out that he took a stick to them when we were away.

Never ignore a dog's warning growl, because that is what it is – a warning, and it must be respected. There is nothing clever or brave about taking a risk with a dog that does not want to be friendly, and this is often the dog that will have to pay the extreme penalty for an unwise and perhaps unwarranted bite, which need never have happened.

OTHER PETS

If you have other pets at home, it is important to supervise introductions. Take special care if you already have a dog – it is all too easy to make a fuss of the puppy, and to make your existing dog feel jealous.

Allow the puppy and the adult to sort out their own relationship, and do not be too swift to punish the adult for a warning growl. The puppy will understand what is meant, and he needs to learn to respect the older dog.

Puppies always want to investigate other species of animals but will soon realise when the canine physical attributes are out-classed. It is quite possible for outdoor animals, such as goats or pot bellied pigs, for example, to become friendly with dogs.

Chapter Five

PUPPY
EDUCATION

We speak here of what you will want to teach your new puppy, but all these commands can be taught to an older dog too. The saying 'you cannot teach an old dog new tricks' is palpably untrue. A willing dog, that has confidence in you and enough incentives offered to make complying with your requests worthwhile in doggy terms, will always learn what you want to teach him. On your part, you must have the patience and consistency of purpose to teach sympathetically and well.

Although we admire the precision of Obedience dogs which we see giving demonstrations at canine events, many of us

A well-behaved dog is a pleasure to own.

Photo: McGovern.

will feel that it is unnecessary for our family dog to attain these standards, and we may not have the time to devote to this training. However, we do need our dog to behave reasonably well at home and when out, so we must teach a few commands in order to control him and to make him an acceptable pet wherever he goes.

The commands we do teach must be obeyed perfectly, with precision, every time. Gradually, you will find that you do not have to give the commands any more – your dog will know intuitively what you want him to do – for instance, going into the sit position when you stop to talk to someone in the street.

Your dog must come when called (See *Recall page 171*), and this must always be obeyed, whether within the house or outside. He must also know the 'Sit' (See *Sit page 186*) and 'Down' (See *Down page 128*) (meaning lie full length) commands, which serve to calm the dog and make him easier to examine. He must walk in a controlled manner on the lead (See *Lead, Leash, Lead training pages 157*), which should be automatic behaviour when the lead is put on, and he should obey the command to 'Get in your bed', for when you need to get him out of the way. You will also make very frequent use of the command you have chosen to direct your dog for elimination purposes.

Your dog will soon find these commands become a way of life which has to be obeyed, provided you are consistent in requiring the behaviour indicated. Often, dogs associate a certain place with a certain behaviour. We keep a tube of peppermint candies on a shelf just inside a bathroom, and it is not unusual to find a row of dogs arranged like statues in classical 'sits' across the doorway, waiting for a reward which might be forthcoming, because this is the situation in which this reward is given.

It is useful to have a little training session just before the dog is fed. When he is hungry, he will be more eager for the food reward you are offering, he will be more focused upon you as meal time draws near. If you tell your dog to do something, persist until the required action is carried out. Sometimes dogs will be rebellious; this can be especially true of male dogs at adolescence. You may find that, on occasion, the dog will refuse to obey, thinking that he knows better, and maybe he does. There may be an intruder in the garden, either animal or human, and your dog is barking non-stop because he thinks you should know about it. We have to admit that very often the dog is right.

CAR TRAVEL

Most dogs love to ride in cars; their best reward is to be accompanying their owners and family. Get your puppy used to the car from the earliest days with you; for a few days, let the puppy explore the car when it is in the garage or some other really safe area. Sit in the car with the pup, with the engine off, and reward the puppy when he is relaxed about doing this. If you feed the puppy in the car, this will make him eager to get into the vehicle when you really want him to.

Once the puppy accepts sitting in the back of the car with the engine running, you are on your way to creating a canine motorist, but he still has to learn for himself how to balance while riding so that he does not fall over at every corner. This accomplishment will come with time, but you should be driving very sedately for the first few weeks with a canine passenger.

You may decide that, for a small dog, the easiest ride will be if you obtain a folding crate that will fit into the back of the car. This has the advantage of keeping the dog in his place, and you can also throw a sheet over the crate to prevent him from getting excited about passing traffic or dogs walking along the pavement. However, you must always be aware that the dog may easily become overheated in a covered crate.

You may want to fit the car with pull-down blinds or some other window cover for use in summer, bearing in mind that dogs feel the heat more than we do, as they can only pant to lose heat – dogs do not sweat as humans do. Excitement or apprehension will also raise the temperature. Ice and plenty of cold water should always be carried in the summer months, as well as a towel, which you can soak in cold water to wrap the dog in if it becomes overheated.

The larger dog has got to stay on the back seat, come what may. There are car harnesses obtainable that can be attached to the seat belt fittings, but simple training to 'sit' and 'down'

Most dogs love a trip out in the car.

Photo: Steph Holbrook.

is usually enough. It can be useful to fill the floor of the rear
seats with some padding, so that the dog is not hurt if he is
shunted off the seat. Where there are two or more dogs to
carry, it is useful to create some boxes that bring the footwells
up to the level of the seat, so that the dogs have the advantage
of a larger flat space. Metal dog guards to fence off the back
seat from the front are practical and sensible, but the guard
must exactly fit your car so that it never collapses or gets out
of place. Most suppliers cater for all models of popular makes
of car. Having a dog guard prevents the dog landing on the
driver's shoulders, either from a rush of affection or in an
accident.

Finally, never leave your dog in the car if the weather is at
all warm and humid, even for a short time and even with the
window open. You may be detained longer than you think,
and in that time your dog could become seriously distressed
or even die of heat stroke. You would never forgive yourself,
so do not ever take the risk that could make this terrible event
become true for you and yours.
(See Car and Travel page 101)

GOOD BEHAVIOUR FOR DOG OWNERS
The most essential quality for any dog owner is to like and
respect dogs. Good owners will:
• Never acquire a dog just as an attention-getting
  accessory.
• Be willing to adapt some parts of their life in the interest
  of the dog.
• Be prepared to accept and understand the nature of the
  dog and never to reject his affection.
• Have the interest to notice the fine details of the dog's
  changing facial expression and behaviour patterns,
  especially those that may denote discomfort or
  unhappiness.
• Have the interest and humility to regard the dog as
  another being worthy of respect for his own heredity and
  talents.
• Always take precautions to prevent the dog getting into
  trouble and to provide for all his needs in sickness and in
  health.
• Have the time and patience to care for a sick or elderly
  dog.
• Appreciate that the dog/human partnership is for the life
  of the dog.

- Always consider the dog when making their own arrangements.
- Always be ready to seek professional veterinary advice if the dog has pain or discomfort.
- Prevent their dog annoying or being a nuisance to other people.
- Remember the countryside code and avoid walking with a dog, even on the lead, alongside or among farm livestock.
- Not allow their dog to chase deer or game birds.
- Keep the dog on the lead on any road or lane used by cars or farm vehicles, however quiet it may seem.

THE GOOD CITIZEN TEST

This is a scheme which started in the USA, and has now been adopted by many national Kennel Clubs. It is based on a series of exercises which will teach a dog the basic elements of canine good manners so that it is acceptable to other members of the public.

See Good Citizens, page 140.

The responsibility for owning a well-adjusted, well-behaved dog lies with the owner. Photo: Steve Nash.

Chapter Six

UNDERSTANDING CANINE BEHAVIOUR

We must never forget that this is an animal we have taken into our homes; not a wild animal, but neither is he a furry-coated mini-human nor a bronze model. Dogs have a number of natural habits that they will continue to practise, no matter what we feel about them. If a dog is reprimanded, say, for licking his rear end, the dog will continue to clean itself in this way, but will make sure the owner is not looking. Dogs do not seem to take into account the fact that the particular noises that such activities create are very audible to us, so we can still say "No!" and surprise the dog by our powers of detection.

LICKING

Dogs lick people, too. They seem to think it their duty to lick at any scratches and sores we may have, and at one time the lick of a dog was thought to be healing. Affectionate dogs also like to 'kiss' people's faces, and this is not always welcome, especially when a heavy Bullmastiff jumps up in order to give a welcoming kiss. That handy word 'No',

Dogs lick instinctively, and this habit should be curbed, with a firm command and a food reward.

Photo: Keith Allison.

an order to sit plus a reward for doing so will calm the moment. Some dogs seem to have a compulsion to lick textiles, the chair covers, and the carpet. It is possible that this is connected with some digestive disorder, which should be investigated.

SNIFFING
Dogs sniff objects, other dogs, and people – that is the way they get their information. They like to go over shoes and clothing when their owner returns from an outing; a pet dog will sniff over your clothes, and seems to be particularly eager to do so when you have met or caressed another dog. Sniffing at visitors can be embarrassing, and the only remedy is to distract the dog with something more interesting, otherwise he will continue to sniff at intimate places until he has found out all he wants to know.

SNORING
Dogs snore, indeed they do, both the short-nosed breeds and those with longer noses. Far from being intrusive, that deep-asleep snore can be very comforting for lonely people, and yet we know that the dog will be instantly alert if anything unexpected happens.

SCRATCHING
Dogs scratch, furiously sometimes. In response to an intense

The dog has a highly sophisticated sense of smell, and sniffing is an absorbing pastime.
                    Photo: Steph Holbrook.

itch, they will often tear their own skin quite badly. There are numerous parasites which can get in between the dog's toes, and the sound of chewing at the feet is quite repulsive. When a dog's feet are sore and itch badly, the owner's help is vital, to bathe the feet and also get rid of the parasite causing the itch.

FLATULENCE

Dogs are quite uninhibited about giving vent to flatulence, and when your dog does so when you are entertaining visitors, the embarrassment is acute. Elderly dogs seem to be more prone to this involuntary emission, and it may be that your vet can suggest a more suitable diet, which does not contain so much gas-producing material.

GRAZING

Dogs graze on grass – sometimes on meadow grass, and sometimes on the expensive ornamental grasses you bought for the garden. The coarse rye grass which dogs sometimes seem to need so urgently is thought to be a digestive aid. Dogs will vomit a ball of it up again quite soon after they have eaten it; perhaps it rids them of some accumulated mucous in the digestive tract.

Some coarse grass will go right through the digestive system and be voided in a neat bolus, but sometimes the grass ends do not clear the rectum entirely. Most dogs are infuriated by the sensation of having a residue of grass protruding from the anus, and will rush about trying to get rid of the appendage, and, in doing so, will apply his offending back end on carpets, cushions and the like. This is not bad behaviour, but merely an animal trying to do what is best for itself. The only practical remedy is for the owner to come to the rescue and to grasp the offending ends in a tissue and pull gently. The dog is always very grateful. In the early spring, when the first bite of new grass comes through, dogs will graze like sheep or cattle. This grass seems to be entirely digested and may be genuinely needed after a long winter. (*See Grass-eating page 142*)

VOMITING

Dogs vomit very easily; they may eat their food very quickly, then vomit it back covered in saliva, and then eat it again with every evidence of pleasure. It is more common for dogs to do this when they feel harried for some reason while eating.

There need be no illness involved, although when water is vomited back there is cause for concern.

BARKING

Dogs normally bark and howl, and we can be very glad that they do. We value that warning bark – perhaps that is partly why we keep dogs. But barking can get too much; the dog can be annoying and disturbing to other people. Dogs have many different barks they can use – the 'asking for' bark, the warning about strangers bark, the 'I got shut in here by mistake' bark, the 'let me out' bark, the 'come on, it's play time' bark, the 'it's meal time' bark, the 'there is something very strange in the garden' bark, the 'help, it's all too much for me' bark...the range is endless. Learn to read your dog's barks, so that you can identify the reason for prolonged barking, and find out if your assistance is needed to repel whatever threat the dog has perceived.
See Barking page 90.

BEHAVIOURAL CHANGES

Dogs are sentient animals, and their behaviour can be influenced to many factors. For instance, weather conditions, puberty and hormonal surges, changes within the family home, illness and therapeutic treatments, old age, and changes in the behaviour of family members including acute sadness or rows, quarrels and violence between humans. All these changes can affect a dog whose life is centred upon watching, listening and eventually comforting distressed family members.

CLIMATIC CONDITIONS

Dogs are often quieter and less responsive to invitations to play or training when the weather is grey, damp or humid. Like wild animals, they will sleep for 22 out of 24 in uninviting weather.

Many dogs, especially those with heavy coats, will be extremely lethargic in hot weather, as they lack the ability to cool themselves as humans can. No attempt should be made to entice the dog to play or to submit to training, except late in the evening and early in the morning, and all car travel with the dog should be restricted to these times.

Cold weather does not seem to affect most dogs; only those that are very old will huddle close to a source of heat all day. High winds excite some dogs – they rush about, enjoying the

Behaviour may be affected by hormones, illness, age, insecurity, and even changes in climate.

wind in their coat, and seem exhilarated. The noise of the wind and cracking of tree branches can worry more nervous dogs. Many people believe that dogs can predict the onset of a storm, but in the noise-laden world we live in now, few dogs take much notice.

There must always be some doubt as to whether dogs were ever afraid of thunder and lightening, or is the fear owner-induced? It is very easy to create a fear of harmless things in a dog – they soon acquire their owners' phobias. If their owner is in mortal fear of a sparrow sitting on the draining board, the dog will feel the need to express a similar fear of a harmless little bird that would warrant no canine attention if it were outside.

Coincidentally, the need to jolly their dog along in the face of an unreasonable fear can cure the owner's phobia too. Dog owners should try not to show fear, so that they create fearless dogs instead of dogs that cower under the table because of an unfamiliar noise.

ADOLESCENCE

The onset of puberty in a male puppy brings possibly the greatest temperament change. Late in a puppy's first year or early in the second year, according to breed, the young male will often demonstrate an urgent desire to mount some object and to go through mating movements. The object may be a human leg, or something inanimate like a sofa cushion, or even a long-suffering household cat. This behaviour can be embarrassing, especially when inflicted on visitors. The cause is an upsurge of the male hormone, testosterone, in the adolescent animal.

The word 'No', to which you have already accustomed the puppy, will serve well here, and so will distracting the puppy with a toy or food. But, it must be admitted that with some male pups, the abortive urge to copulate will take precedence over everything else for a few weeks or months. You will find that even if there is a bitch living in the home, he will not try to mate with her, just because she will not allow it. She will tell him in no uncertain terms to go away; and he will obey her, just as he used to obey his dam, because he really is a bit afraid of mature bitches.

Do not be tempted to arrange to use your young dog at stud. For one thing, there will probably be no takers unless he has been tested for fertility. If you do provide a mating experience for him, it may well be the one and only time in his life that it happens for him, because the vast majority of breeders want to use dogs that have won at shows.

Your young male may get the urge to escape, and be constantly going off to look for co-operative bitches, so that you will not be the most popular dog owner in the area. During this adolescent stage, your male dog is going to be somewhat of a nuisance, but it will pass, I do assure you, and if you succeed in controlling your dog through this phase, you will have more authority over him hereafter. If you find the dog really impossible to live with, consult your vet about the various chemical and surgical means by which over-sexed dogs can be controlled.

OLD AGE
Old age can have a dramatic effect on a dog's behaviour, as can any illness or medication that affects the brain. Some breeds may become senile and suffer from age disabilities at seven to eight years old, while Collie breeds, Spaniels and

Be considerate to the veteran who will have special needs as she grows older.

many mongrels may retain their youthful attributes well into their teens. One noticeable feature of dogs feeling their age is that they easily become disorientated. They will run surprisingly fast in completely the wrong direction. Their sight fails and they become deaf. They may sometimes be urine incontinent, and they may make mistakes about defecation through inability to get outside in time because of severe arthritic pain when trying to rise from a lying position.

An older dog needs a great deal of observation, patience and care, because what may appear to be disobedience may in fact be a physical failing, which it may be possible to alleviate in a number of ways. Ask for your veterinarian's advice.

HEREDITARY DEAFNESS

At the other end of the age scale, there is the possibility that your newly acquired puppy may have been born with partial or complete hereditary deafness. This can happen in any breed, but some breeds, especially Dalmatians, white Bull Terriers, white Boxers and Border Collies with predominantly white coats, as well as coloured individuals in other breeds, may be affected by hereditary deafness in one or both ears. Breeders should have breeding stock tested before they are mated, and puppies should be tested for hearing disability before they are sold. There is a scientific test now available, called the Brainstem Auditory Evoked Reaction (the BAER test) which uses computer technology.

The test is painless and can be used upon puppies from about five weeks old. It shows accurately the amount of sound that reaches each of the pup's ears. If the test is not available at your veterinary practice, your veterinary surgeon will be able to refer you to a practice that has this equipment.

The more informal way of testing for deafness has traditionally been to drop a metal bowl behind the puppy and to watch his reactions, or to clap your hands loudly and see if the pup is aware of the noise. You may become suspicious of deafness if the pup fails to respond to training. Perhaps, earlier in the training, the puppy may have been good at coming when called because of the welcoming gestures you made – getting down on your haunches and opening your arms wide encouraged him to make contact with you. This was, in effect, training by means of hand signals, and not by voice.

Do not despair if your puppy or adult dog is found to be

*Some breeds,
such as
Dalmatians,
are more likely
to be affected
by hereditary
deafness.*

*Photo: Carol
Ann Johnson.*

deaf because it is possible to train a totally deaf dog to respond to hand signals. Training a dog that has little or no hearing inevitably requires even more patience and application than training a hearing one, but it is a very rewarding thing to do, creating, as it does, a very special bond between dog and owner.

If you find that your puppy is deaf, it is important that you inform the breeder so that the pup's sire and dam are not be bred from again. While admitting that it can be difficult to identify a deaf puppy when he is with the litter (one pup follows the others), breeders who know that deafness affects their breed should be aware of possible problems. It places a huge emotional burden on a puppy buyer to find he has acquired a puppy, which has become part of their family, and then to find that training is going to require even more time, patience and skill than normal. Only a minority of people will meet this challenge, and most pups found to be deaf will, it is sad to say, be destroyed, because there is no way to restore or create the ability to hear in a dog.

THE SEASONAL CYCLE
Bitches come into season for the first time possibly at about a year old, or maybe nearer two years old depending on size. The approaching oestrus period may be signalled by a temporary development of a more excitable nature. You will also notice swelling of the vulva and a white or opaque discharge. which will gradually become infused with blood. This is the bitch in season (in oestrus) for real.

As a bitch is capable of mating at her first season, she will increase urine marking in order to send the message to all available males. An in-season bitch is best kept on your own premises and not taken out at all, so that you can reduce the annoyance brought on by free-running males. She may keep herself clean, but short-coated breeds do create a certain amount of staining from the blood-coloured discharge, so you will want to protect your carpets and furnishings. Do not, however, banish the bitch from the family circle – she needs company and affection as much as ever. It has been known for family members to sit in the utility room in the evenings and to do their homework there in order to be with the bitch. Reckon on the season lasting about a month in all, although the red discharge will cease earlier than this.

PHANTOM PREGNANCY

The bitch has another and even more significant behaviour change with which to surprise you. Because the hormonal changes are the same whether a bitch has been mated or not, many entire bitches, and even some spayed ones, go through some degree of phantom pregnancy, when they act as though they have actually produced a litter. Phantom pregnancies can differ widely; spayed bitches will probably show only a mild depression and lack of appetite for a few days. Some bitches, however, will go through a real performance of tearing up paper and blankets to make a whelping bed, mimicking labour pains and then cleaning and caring for some small objects, toys, or even, in one household, small kitchen utensils as substitutes for puppies. Bitches who put their all into a phantom pregnancy may even bring themselves into milk to feed the puppies that are not really there.

The problem with phantom pregnancies is that the bitch may become really serious about protecting this litter that no-one else can see, and a stranger sitting down in an armchair to which the bitch has just moved her invisible puppies may get the full force of the bitch's wrath. It is important to keep children away from her at this time as her temperament may have altered drastically, but the episode will not last for long. Look after the bitch well and do give her more food than is normal, provide more exercise and do not sympathise with her. Jolly her out of a phantom pregnancy, but do not promise her a real pregnancy next time. It is not that she longs for puppies, but just that her hormones have got out of control. Your bitch will return to her own sweet self in two or three weeks, much less time than an actual litter would take to rear. Your vet can help if the situation becomes impossible to handle.

FAMILY DISRUPTION

Our dogs are much more aware of our own state of mind and tensions within the house than we give them credit for. Serious quarrels between family members, shouting, crashing out and slamming doors can upset a sensitive dog. Depression, lack of appetite and lethargy may be some of the symptoms the dog shows. He will do his canine best to comfort someone in tears, but misery is infectious, and the dog gets it too. Where a couple eventually part company, their dog may be badly affected, because he was loyal and devoted to both parties.

Dogs can be temperamental, too, and show all too clearly that they are not pleased with alterations that have taken place within the family circle. A dog will often miss the children terribly when they go back to school after long holidays, and he may badly resent new residents in the home, especially if they are non-doggy people, possibly elderly and requiring a lot of care and attention. Dogs are all too capable of jealousy, but this mood is shown in depression and lethargy, and very rarely in bad temper. A dog will not be jealous of a new baby, provided he gets just as much attention as he always had and is also allowed to participate in interaction with the baby.

Dogs do resent being shut away when non-doggy visitors are being entertained, but resentment will be forgotten if some special treat, such as a good game with his owners, a special run or a ride in the car is provided immediately after the visitors have taken their departure. Let the good things happen!

CORRECTING BAD BEHAVIOUR

Inevitably, there will be times when temptation overcomes conditioning and training and you need to apply a deterrent while the dog is in the act of digging a plant up in the garden, bullying the cat, trying to jump the boundary, or whatever youthful mischief a dog can devise.

A water pistol kept filled and handy or a beanbag which comes easily to hand are your best friends here. Direct the stream of water, the beanbag or any other thrown object to land beside the dog, and not to hit him directly. The real secret is that the retribution for the crime does not come from you, the beloved owner, or from any other member of the family – it comes out of the blue from the great Dog Star in the sky. If you have no suitable throwing object when you need it, a crashing noise, such as banging metal upon metal, or clapping your hands sharply serves to alert the dog to his wrongdoing.

See Aversion page 87.

FEAR

Sometimes events may occur that cause real fear and uncharacteristic behaviour in a dog which normally has a very steady and reliable character. Following a relatively minor car accident in a country lane, my husband's dog Tigger leapt out through the shattered windscreen and disappeared into the surrounding countryside. He was nowhere to be seen and made no response to calling – behaviour totally uncharacteristic in this dog.

At last, three or four hours later, we were told he was lying on the edge of some woodland, but when we walked towards him, he ran away from us. Apparently, just before the crash occurred, Tigger had moved over into the front passenger seat, where he was normally forbidden to be, and we surmised that he thought the bang and being thrown off the seat was a violent punishment, something he had never experienced before. Although Tigger would not come to us, he did not go far away, and eventually my husband sat down in the field and pleaded, very passively, with the dog to come to him.

After quite a long time, when dusk was falling, Tigger came to realise that we meant him no harm, and he crept, slowly and cautiously, back to my husband, whose dog he was. When our car came back repaired, Tigger utterly refused to get into it. He would get into a rented car, or anyone else's car, but it was a long time before he trusted that orange Mini again, but eventually he did come to enjoy his rides as much as he did before. The moral of this little story is never to force a dog to face such a fear. A quiet appreciation of all that the dog must be feeling will, in the end, bring the dog round.

THE POWER TO RESPOND

You and your dog can have an extraordinary depth of feeling for each other and you can forge bonds that are like no other. Dogs that are shut away and ignored lose their power to respond. Keep the contact which you made with the new puppy, talk to and pat your dog in passing, play games with your dog and always respond when the dog himself suggests a game by bringing you one of his toys. Keep your dog's intelligence alive all the time by providing new experiences, and above all, by talking to your dog.

SECTION II

A-Z OF DOG TRAINING AND BEHAVIOUR

An alphabetical listing of terms, methods and definitions.

By Patrick Holden

A

ACTING DOGS
See Media, page 160

AGE – Dogs
Instructors are often asked at what age puppies should start being trained. The modern answer is "the sooner the better".

STAGES OF DEVELOPMENT

Basic Control: Rather than formal training, it is preferable to shape behaviour from the outset as a puppy. *(See Basic Control, page 91).* One example is the Recall. Shape your puppy to come to you by using his name and the word "Come" every time you have a food dish in your hand. At other times, the other rewards – praise (always) a pat, a treat, a toy or a game – will ensure that your puppy is shaped to come to you his handler as he is called. Behaviour shaping is used in many of the training exercises outlined within the 'A-Z' listing.

Competition: A minimum age for competing in some sports is stipulated by the various national regulatory bodies e.g. six months in Obedience, and eighteen months in Working Trials and Agility. The rationale for this is that the dog's bones should be matured and his body should be generally capable of attempting Agility and Working Trials obstacles.

Maturity: Different breeds of dog mature at different times. Some of the larger breeds do not mature until they are over eighteen months, while others may mature before a year old. Handlers should consider not only physical maturity but also the mental maturity of the dog. It is important to be concerned about your dog's bones and joints, but you must also consider whether your dog – and come to that, you the handler – are mentally ready.

Retirement: At the other end of the age spectrum, it is more difficult to judge when dogs should be stopped. Enthusiastic dogs who love games are often the last ones to know that they are getting 'past it'. A handler and his trainer need to look for the telltale signs. These are, of course, very evident in speed sports, but the signs are less obvious in the jumping sports, when like older human athletes, a dog takes longer to recover from sprains and other injuries.

It is difficult to generalise but, here again, the larger, heavier breeds tend to retire sooner than those with a lighter build. A case in point was a Border Collie which won a ranking championship in Obedience in 1998 aged almost twelve. Other dogs may be too old at seven. Handlers and their instructors must be alert to make these difficult decisions.

It is a myth that you cannot teach an old dog new tricks. For example, a dog going deaf in later years can be successfully retrained to follow hand signals. *(See Body language, page 97)* . Even when you have to stop competition, you must not, of course, stop games with your beloved dog.

AGE – Handlers

The age at which to start (and stop) human handlers is also often asked. In relation to dogs, whether as pets or in dog sports, we are more fortunate than in many other occupations, sporting or otherwise. Dog owning can start early and go on to any age. Dog ownership has been scientifically proved to prolong human life.

With regard to starting competition, as with most other sports, the younger and sooner the better. The UK Kennel Club has instituted its excellent Kennel Club Junior Organisation (KCJO), and the American Kennel Club has its AKCJO to help youngsters start properly and prepare to climb the competition ladder. *(See Kennel Club Junior Organisation, page 156).*

The Good Citizenship Scheme in the UK and the Canine Good Citizen Program in the US have been designed to cover both dogs and handlers of all ages. *(See Good Citizens, page 140).*

With regard to the older generation, it is possible for

handlers to compete successfully even into their seventies – a great boon compared to other sports. Indeed, the author who is the wrong side of sixty certainly hopes to go for a few more years yet! *Old dogs can learn new tricks...*

AGGRESSION
Aggression on the part of a dog is of major concern, particularly in this increasingly anti-dog age. It is shown by barking, growling, teeth baring and, at worst, biting.

Aggression shows itself in different forms, but in adult dogs it cannot be tolerated.

Photo: John Daniels.

It is important to identify the causes of such aggression. Remember that dogs are descended from wolves. Among the wolf characteristics are the need to get food, which obviously means bringing down and killing prey, i.e. with aggression, but also that of surviving in a pack i.e. without aggression.

Some breeds are more 'aggressive' than others and have been so bred, e.g., the guarding breeds – Rottweiler, Dobermann and some of the Terriers. Other breeds tend to be more passive.

Aggression is allied to the dog's defence mechanism. As with many humans, aggression is borne out of defence. It usually starts with a threat or a warning (a bark, growl and then teeth baring) and then moves onward to biting, clawing, and, eventually killing, if there is no option left.

WHAT TRIGGERS AGGRESSION?
The triggers for aggressive behaviour may be attributed to a number of factors. These include the hereditary ones mentioned above, but may also be the result of training, e.g.,

where the dog has been 'trained' aggressively, and/or a lack of socialisation where the dog has not been actively mixed with humans, particularly children and other dogs.

Aggressive behaviour may be apparent when the dog is quite properly defending his perceived territory against strangers – his house, his car, his garden etc. It is also very evident when the dog has been allowed to dominate in its pack. *(See Dominance, page 125)*

COPING WITH AGGRESSION
Aggression is no longer to be tolerated. Dogs have been part of the human pack for so long that they must be trained to conform to human values. This training must include: -
Basic Control: This is an essential for all dogs. *(See Basic Control, page 91)* Shape your dog positively and reinforce him by rewards (praise, treat, game, patting etc. *See Rewards, page 178*). Use the dog's name, and work on:
• Attention: "Watch" then "Close"
• Recall: "Come"
• Positions: "Sit", "Down", "Stand", "In" to car, crate, etc.
• Retrieve: "Hold", "Give", and "Leave".
   With these simple exercises *(see A-Z entries)* you can control your dog both in your home and outside, and thus defuse any potentially aggressive situation.

DOMINANCE REDUCTION: If your dog is dominant and has aggressive traits you must re-shape him by a dominance reduction programme. *(See Dominance, page 125)*
Diversion: *(see page 122)* Watch and learn your dog's body language: if his hackles are up, he is on his toes and stiff-legged, baring his teeth and growling then he is aggressive. Use Basic Control: call him back to you, and put him to the Down – the submissive posture.
Prevention: Protect yourself, your family and others. Contain him:
Outdoors: Always use a collar and lead. Contain him with a muzzle.
Indoors: Use the crate, or muzzle him before visitors enter.
Physical: Consider neutering in males. This almost always results in a reduction in both dominance and aggression.

AGILITY
Agility is one of the newer dog sports. It is akin to show-jumping with the dog having to complete a course,

clearing various obstacles against the clock. It is now a fully-fledged and highly competitive sport in its own right. It is fun for competitors – both handlers and dogs – and it is also a great spectator sport.

Agility is a fun sport for both dog and handler.

Photo: Keith Allison.

Although the handler does not touch the dog during the competition, it is a team exercise. A crafty handler, by judicious choice of position, can reduce the amount he has to move. Nevertheless, a competition is a time trial, and the handler has to be in the right spot to give the correct command to ensure that the dog covers all the obstacles in as short a time as possible. Both dog and handler must be fit!

Anyone wanting to compete in Agility should join an appropriate club. It is even more essential in Agility than in other sports because of the specialist equipment and the space required. Joining a club will also ensure you and your dog receive tuition and insurance cover in case of accident.

WHEN TO START?
Dogs are not allowed to compete in Agility until they are eighteen months of age (when growth is completed). However, you should not start Agility training until your dog has mastered Basic Control *(see page 91)*. This means that your dog must be able to respond to "Sit", "Down", "Wait", "Come" (Recall) instantaneously on command. Sendaway *(see page 182)* is helpful, as is Retrieve *(see page 175)*. Most Agility Clubs do not offer courses on Basic Control and it is, therefore, essential that you should acquire these skills, preferably by learning them at an Obedience Club and/or by videos, reading books, and studying other related material.

For reasons of safety, the beginner handler must use the Agility Club's obstacles, and this must only be in the presence of a competent instructor. Your equipment must include a double lead (two leads linked together) and a hoop. Agility is a speed sport for handler as well as dog, so you will need trainers/sneakers and a track suit or equivalent.

GENERAL PRINCIPLES
The principles are the same as in other canine sports.
• Break each exercise into its element, then train each element separately.
• Only train the elements together when each has been mastered.
• Use the Aids: *(see page 81)* voice (command and praise), hands to demonstrate and pat, the lead (one or two together), treats and/or a toy.
• Emphasise behaviour shaping by correct teaching and understanding.
• Reinforce by giving reward rather than correction or compulsion.
• Ensure both dog and handler are fit.

CONTACT POINTS
It is essential that your dog understands that he must touch the contact point (the yellow strip at each end of the relevant obstacles). Try the following measures to achieve this:
• Train your dog to go through a hand-held hoop. Hold the hoop before each point and call your dog through it (particularly A Frame and Walkway).
• Instant "Down" on each contact (particularly the See-saw).
• Reward on each contact point (treat initially and then praise).
• Try combining all three exercises.

THE OBSTACLES
Outline training is given to provide an idea of what is required. The contact equipment should be trained in the following order: A Frame, See-saw, Walkway.
A Frame: Guide your dog up on the lead. Use the toy as an incentive (on double lead, drawn upwards), command "Walk on". Alternatively, the instructor holds your dog at the bottom while the handler climbs up the other side and recalls. Try both!
Seesaw: Train before the Walkway. Start with a plank on the

Take time with the early stages of training so your dog will develop confidence.   *Photo: Keith Allison.*

ground then raised on one brick. The dog should be on a lead and the handler gives the command: "Walk on". Take time and continue working until the dog is comfortable. Next, one end as a slope, thus teaching the descent first, then reverse to ascent.

Now use the Seesaw with the handler encouraging the dog on, and instructor holding it level. When at fulcrum, the instructor gently lowers the rear end. The handler should encourage the dog to go down using the aids. The instructor's intervention (balancing the Seesaw) should be reduced so that the dog learns the fulcrum. Train contact points separately (see above).

Walkway: Train in full only after the Seesaw (otherwise your dog may become nervous of heights). Break into elements and train each element separately: going up; along; going down. The command is "Walk on". Only progress when your dog thoroughly understands all three elements. Train contact points with the handler on the left and the right. Build up speed gradually.

Jumps: There are two main types: the 'over' jump (clear hurdle, brick wall and spread) – and the 'through' jump (tyre/hoop and wishing well).

Over jump: Start with low pole with your dog on lead. Walk over the pole and command "Over", then repeat at the run. Use the aids, then raise the pole. Walk over, then run as before. Progress gradually, training off-lead. If your dog hesitates, goes through or knocks down the pole go back a stage. A toy thrown over the pole can be used as an incentive aid.

Through jump: Train with a hoop (see also Contact Points) and aids both at ground level. Command "Through" then raise the hoop. When your dog becomes proficient, increase the height. Ensure you train each element slowly so that the dog understands what is required.

Table: Your dog has to jump on to a table, go down for five seconds before proceeding. A table is useful for basic training and control, to teach your pup distant control, for grooming and for examination *(see Table page 195)*, and so this should already be a familiar object. When starting with a puppy, lift the pup on to the table. Then use an intermediate box as a step, and finally encourage the dog to jump up. Command "Table". Use the aids, particularly the toy as an incentive, then as a reward for success. In the unlikely event of these tips not working, the handler must get on the table himself and recall the dog up. Use the "Down" and "Stay" elements.

Weave: Start with the weave poles placed in two lines, alternating with the poles angled outwards. Walk your dog through on his short lead several times. Then place his toy at the end as an incentive. Command "Weave".

Gradually slope the angles of the poles until they are vertical, and reduce the space between the poles progressively until they are in a straight line. Continue the incentive, but vary the use of the lead. Reward when your dog comes through the weave. Make sure your dog thoroughly masters weaving with the poles vertical before increasing speed gradually.

Tunnels - Fixed And Collapsible: Train with the hoop initially. When your dog is proficient at this, the instructor should hold the dog at mouth of the tunnel (the training for both types of tunnel is the same). The hander holds the other end of the tunnel open, showing the toy and recalling the dog with the "Through" command. Later on, the instructor and handler should reverse roles. Use the "Wait" element at the mouth of the tunnel.

PUTTING IT TOGETHER

Only when both you and your dog are proficient with individual obstacles (element training), should you progress to pairs of obstacles, and small courses. Start off tackling obstacles in straight lines, and when you are proficient, introduce turns between obstacles. Teach handling with your dog on both left and right hand-side. Use turn directions "Left" and "Right".

Advanced training is now required to achieve the speed and accuracy required at competition level.

A

AIDS
This term is used when referring to the 'help' a handler can give a dog when teaching an exercise or when shaping behaviour. It originates from schooling horses, and although some of the 'aids' are similar, the canine world has now developed its own system.

Most of the aids used today are also rewards. The best aid for dog training is your voice (always remember the praise before the blame). Other rewards include: a small food treat, the clicker *(see Clicker Training page 108)*, a toy, a game, physical praise - stroking, patting, and body language *(see page 97)*. The collar and lead are vital aids – they are many and varied as to type and material *(see Collars, page 111)*.

In the past, negative 'aids' were used which were more in the line of punishment. Thankfully, these are now largely out-moded.

Body language can be both positive and negative. Dogs are far more sensitive to body language than people. You can influence your dog from being joyful and tail-wagging if you look happy and excited, to making him dismal and depressed when you frown and slump. Identify, and use, the aids which work particularly well for you.

ALLERGY
Both dogs and humans suffer allergic reactions. While their cause and cure are beyond the remit of this book*, handlers must be on their guard for the signs of allergic reactions. Not only do they affect the dog's behaviour in training and competition or elsewhere but they are, of course, of discomfort to the dog.

Human allergies may be dealt with by medicaments e.g. antihistamine. In other cases, it is simpler to separate the sufferer from the dog. With puppies and, indeed, older dogs this is where the crate or pen comes into its own. A stairgate may also be a help during visits. To prevent your dog always associating visitors, or this particular visitor, with a bad experience, always give a pleasurable diversion, e.g., a chew.

*See A-Z of Dog Diseases and Health Problems, published in the UK by Ringpress Books, and in North America by Howell Book House.

AMERICAN KENNEL CLUB (AKC)
The USA's leading authority, and regulating body, for purebred dogs.

The AKC aims to provide a service and a source of information for all those interested in pedigree (purebred) dogs, whether in canine sports or purely as companions. Its mission statement is to:-

• Maintain a registry for purebred dogs and preserve its integrity.
• Sanction dog events that promote interest in and sustain the process of breeding for type and function of purebred dogs.
• Take whatever action is necessary to protect and assure the continuation of the sport of purebred dogs.

The AKC runs well over 1000 Breed shows each year, with over 1.5 million dogs in competition. Other events include Obedience (approx. 1000 Trials p.a.), Agility (approx. 300 Trials), Earthdog events, Hunting tests (with over 50,000 participants).

Its services include a Library, Clubs Relations Department and it supports the AKC Museum and the AKC Health Foundation.
See Addresses, page 208.

ANTHROPOMORPHISM
This is a term beloved of dog psychologists and behaviourists. It simply means ascribing human characteristics to a dog.

With over six million dogs in Great Britain and more than 20 million in the USA, it is not surprising that some pets are given a higher status in their human surroundings than they would have enjoyed in the wild. Some dogs have become child substitutes; there is the owner who believes that his/her pet "understands every word I say", or "he knows what I'm thinking", or "he's so intelligent", etc.

Dogs do not have the same emotions as humans. They do not have the same powers of reasoning. They are intelligent, but their intelligence differs from that of humans. The canine mind is much less cluttered and far more direct than humans. They are very sensitive to body language whether human or animal. For example:

• Dogs do not get excited at Christmas or Thanksgiving because of the festival; they get excited because their human owners are excited.
• It is not usually love that makes a dog nudge his owner, it is an attention-seeking device.
• A dog is not punishing his owner after returning from kennels if he appears to be in a decline. Such a dog has often received privileges of rank in his human pack which are far greater than he would have received in a dog pack. If this dog is kennelled with other dogs when his owners go away, his status is diminished. On returning home, the dog adopts the more submissive demeanour of a sub-ordinate member. In this instance, the owners should look at how they rate their dog, and, more importantly, how the dog rates his own place in the human pack.

Remember, DOG must never be spelt backwards!

ANXIETY
Dogs, who do not have the human powers of reasoning and logic can, nevertheless, have strong emotional attachments. Dogs express their worries differently from humans.

Problems are shown by behaviour which often causes distress to owners. The symptoms of this behaviour may be focused on one type of behaviour or a combination of different behaviours. These may include: noise (howling and barking), mess (defecation and/or urination in the house), destructiveness, (of furniture and articles within the house

An over-anxious dog will be distressed when his owner is out of sight – even if he is only in the next room.

Photo: Carol Ann Johnson.

including handler's clothing), digging (escape – this can be both in the house and in an outside kennel).

SEPARATION ANXIETY
Behaviourists have identified a particular form of anxiety as separation anxiety. As so often the diagnosis is halfway to the cure. The symptoms of this include:
• Following an owner from room to room.
• Sleeping in the bedroom.
• Trying to get into the bathroom with the owner.
• Scratching on doors or barking when the dog cannot get to owner in the house.
• Showing nervousness at noise, strangers, rustling objects etc.

CHRONIC ASD (Attention Seeking Devices)
These may include:
• Nudging under the arm.
• Resting with his body touching the owner's and gazing into the owner's eyes.
• Trying to sit on the owner's lap.
• Lying with one paw over the owner's feet, as a form of restraint.
   These are signs of an over-attached relationship. The symptoms themselves, and the resulting behaviour, arise because the dog is over-anxious when left alone. The problem shows itself when the owner leaves the dog. The root is the interaction when the owner is actually in the house with the dog.
   Behaviourists have achieved good results in curing anxiety-related problems by reshaping behaviour. This is not only in relation to the dog, it focuses particularly on the owner and their daily routine with the dog.
In the house: If the dog is distressed when he is separated from his owner in the house, then, obviously he will not be happy if the owner leaves the house completely.
   All routines must be changed so that the owner must spend noticeable periods of time in one room with the dog peacefully in another. There is a halfway stage where a stairgate can be used so that the dog can, at least, see his owner. The transition must be gradual, leading to longer periods in separate rooms and eventually with the dog being shut out of the bedroom at night.
   The indoor crate is useful at this stage, and even if the dog

has not been trained to use one, he can still be taught to regard it as his safe haven. *(See Crate training, page 117).* To begin with, the dog can go in his crate when his owner is in the room, then he can go in a separate room where he can still hear voices. He should then spend longer periods in his crate, so he gets used to coping with separation while being in his 'den'.

Leaving home: The greeting and parting routine must be changed. The departures should be as brief as possible. This is where the crate comes into its own, as you can leave the house without a great fuss.

Returning home: Give a warm greeting when you return home, but do not be over-exuberant. Do not react if you return to find that yout dog has fouled or been destructive. While totally understandable, the urge must be resisted as it will simply reinforce the anxiety in the dog. He will not be able to associate the anger and frustration with the soiling and destruction. He will merely relate it to his owner's greeting. This will inevitably lead to more anxiety.

OTHER THERAPIES
• Provide a distraction, such as leaving a television or a radio switched on. You can also leave a safe chewing toy to help keep the dog occupied.
• Some people have found that herbal remedies are helpful, and there is now a clinical remedy, available only through vets, that is designed to reduce stress. These remedies can also be useful in other situations the dog finds stressful, for example travel.

ARTICLES
'Articles' in the dog world refer to articles used for training or in competition to search, find and retrieve.

Articles can be broken down to the following categories:
• In sight: e.g. a dummy in Field Trials, or a dumb-bell in Obedience;
• In sight but requiring discrimination: e.g., scent cloths in Obedience.
• Hidden and searched for blind: e.g., as an exercise in Working Trials and Field Trials, and also in operational training in the Services e.g., drug sniffing, forensic, fires, etc.

GETTING STARTED
Beginner handlers must ensure that the articles used can be safely handled by their dogs. In addition to the dummies etc., already mentioned, you can also use a knotted sock, a length of hosepipe, or a ball on a rope. The article can either be thrown in sight or hidden, and when retrieved, you can reward immediately with a game.

Beginners must not use the small articles used in top competition. For example, in Working Trials these may include a nail, a cut rubber-band, a cork, or a key. All these can cause problems to dogs that are not fully trained. Use appropriate articles.

ATTITUDE
'Attitude' is the term used by dog handlers often with a capital 'A' to describe a dog's approach to life and, in particular, his approach to work or other games.

The collie 'eye' typical of top-class workers.

Photo: Keith Allison.

Attitude refers to the qualities of enthusiasm, professionalism, happiness and aptitude for hard work that are thought desirable for the relevant activities. Examples include:
• The collie 'eye' for sheepdog handling.
• The courage required by police dogs.
• The hard work and stamina needed in dogs picking up after shooting, herding (whether sheep or cattle), operational tracking, or sniffing for drugs.

Dogs with the right Attitude are highly-prized within their working discipline. However, some dogs with these characteristics may not thrive in pet homes. Unless adequately managed by the pack leader, this type of dog may exhibit traits of dominance *(see page 125)*, and may even become aggressive.

AVERSION
Aversion is a technique in a dog handler's armoury to shape behaviour in order to change an unwanted activity. The aim is to create an unpleasant association in the dog's mind with behaviour that is considered undesirable by the handler in the hope that this will stop him from repeating it in the future.

Aversion can be used in conjunction with positive reinforcement methods (treats, games, clicker, etc.), but it is usually used when these methods have failed or been improperly used! Aversion therapy is directed at a dog's senses – those of taste, touch, hearing, and/or sight, and uses the principle of an action producing a reaction.

TASTE
This is used to check unwanted behaviour e.g. chewing. Use a taste that is really unpleasant to your dog like tabasco (or one of the specific products on the market, e.g. bitter apple). Use an old detergent bottle and spray 'flavour' on furniture legs, newspapers, letters, etc., and other items that may be chewed. This therapy has been used to stop retrieving dogs eating birds.

Soak a rag with the taste, and give it to the dog to hold in his mouth, with his jaws closed. He will reject it and endeavour to rid himself of the taste and smell. A dog's sense of smell is at least 100 times better than that of humans, so the dog will remember the unpleasant taste when he next smells it. You may have to repeat the 'hold/taste' once more, but this is not usually necessary.

Another method of taste aversion was used by a handler to stop his dog eating his chickens' eggs. He let some eggs go rotten and then left them for the dog to find and eat. It worked – the dog never stole another egg!

TOUCH
This is used against unwanted behaviour such as barking, chasing or aggression. Water can be very effective – not the pleasant, splashing swim-in stuff – but a well-directed squirt in the dog's face. Use a water-pistol or an old detergent bottle, and direct the spray instantly and accurately at your dog's mouth or face. This usually stops a dog barking or growling.

Other touch aversions include electricity. An electric shock collar should only be used under trained supervision *(see*

Collars page 111). Electric ring fencing systems have been used successfully with an electronic collar, but only when installed by a professional and when the dog has been correctly trained. *(See Containment page 114)*

HEARING
Sound aversion is based on the Pavlovian principle of conditioning reflex to noise.

The principle of using sound for aversion is simple. As the Clicker is a noise device that is used to reinforce action positively *(see Clicker training, page 108)*, so the handler creates a particular noise which will condition a dog to avoid taking the unwanted action. Timing is essential.

The correct noise for this therapy is one which is uncommon. Examples are a tin-can filled with pebbles, a child's rattle, or brass discs – some are purpose-made). The bject chosen must be portable, easy to throw, and with a discrete noise.

Discs are an effective tool when training sound aversion.

Photo courtesy: Dogs Today.

Training
Discs are used here, but the training applies to any of the objects you have chosen.
• Offer the dog a treat. Give the command "Take It".
• Place another treat on the floor with no command. As the dog goes forward to take the treat, drop the discs. Pick up both discs and the treat, and ignore the dog.
• The first time, the dog is likely to seek the treat by sniffing, searching, etc. After a short period, repeat the procedure.
• It usually takes between three to ten repetitions before a dog gets the idea. He will then often take himself off to his den. Basically, he has learnt that the *action* of going for the food without the command creates the *reaction* of the discs

together with the disappearance of the food. Once learnt, this sound can be used to interrupt any other unwanted behaviour.

An example is a dog that charged at the letter box, ate all the letters and cheques – but somehow managed to leave the bills uneaten! Delivery people are 'enemies' to dogs. They invade the dog's territory, and they usually have odd shapes (delivery bags, etc.). However, the dog can 'see them off', defending his territory by barking and charging. Instant success – the intruder goes, and the dog has therefore self-reinforced his own action.

The solution, using disc training, is to:
• Arrange for a third party to come to the house at a specific time, and rattle the letterbox.
• As the dog charges, the handler throws the discs at the door (not at the dog). The dog fails to get any letters, and the noise that he associates with the discs conditions him to return to the handler for praise.
• Repeat the procedure some ten minutes later.
• On the third occasion, letters should be put through the box.
• Thereafter, apply the same technique when the postman himself comes.

Use this technique in other circumstances, not only in the house but also outside. For example, if your dog shows any aggression towards any other dog or human, use of the specific sound should induce the dog to stop his unwanted action and return to the handler for praise and a reward.

Remember, do not use sound aversion for noise-sensitive dogs.
See Clicker Training *(page 108)* for positive sound reinforcement. But unless you are very experienced, do not use both methods with a young dog.

SIGHT
The power of your body language. Dogs are far better at reading us than we realise *(see Body Language page 97)*. Use this principle for both positive shaping and negative aversion.

A dog trained by Basic Control to "Watch" you, will follow your facial expression and body movements. Reward him when he responds to a positive smile and pleased expression, and when he reacts to a negative scowl or glower or even headshake, provided he stops the unwanted action.

B

BACK
"Back" is the command often used by handlers to get a dog to Stand.

The words/commands you use do not matter as long as they are simple, clear and consistent. The advantage of using "Back" is that "Stand" can sound too like "Sit", particularly at a distance. See Stand *(page 190)* for training this exercise.

BARKING
Almost all dogs bark. They communicate warnings, greetings, calls for assistance or attention. However, persistent barking is a nuisance to humans – barking is one of the most frequent complaints about dogs.

Decide on your strategy: do you want your dog to bark a warning, for example:
• When visitors come?
• When 'his' car is touched?
• When you are approached by a stranger outdoors?
• In competition, demonstration, etc.?
   Noise pollution by dogs is now an offence in many jurisdictions *(e.g. see Noise Nuisance for UK law, page 162)*. You must, therefore, shape your dog's barking.

POSITIVE TRAINING
You must train him to bark ("Speak") on command and train him to be ("Quiet") on command. Early basic training is vital. Start as soon as you get your puppy home. Shape him whenever he barks for food, for attention, at a visitor, etc. with the command "Speak", then give him an immediate reward. This is not always easy e.g. when your pup barks excitedly at a stranger at the door, and you reward your puppy with praise.
   Equally train "Quiet". A puppy cannot bark and eat. Have a treat or a toy ready. Offer it to him and as he stops barking, command "Quiet", then reward. At mealtimes, if the puppy barks for his food, command "Speak", and give him a portion of his food. Then if he barks again for the balance, ignore him until he stops. Command "Quiet" and give him his food as a reward.

OTHER TECHNIQUES

If the positive shaping is not being successful, particularly the "Quiet" command, you must review your dog's reason for barking, identify triggers and change your own pack's behaviour. Meanwhile, use:

Diversion *(see page 122 for detailed training)*, but briefly:
• Train "Down". It is more difficult for a dog to bark when he is lying down.
• Train "Hold". If your dog is holding his article correctly he cannot bark as well.
• Combine both.

Aversion *(see page 87 for detailed training)* but briefly:
• Touch. Use the sudden water squirt from your water-pistol or detergent bottle.
• Hearing. Use sound technique with keys, can or discs.
• Sight. Use your face and body language to show disapproval by scowl, frown or loom.

Do not shout, it will only make your dog worse.

BASIC CONTROL
It is essential in today's anti-dog world that you teach your puppy the basic good manners required to ensure that you, your family, your neighbours and friends enjoy your dog.

A puppy is a member of your pack, and he has to learn his place. He must be well-behaved, without losing his natural characteristics. You must teach him not to damage people or possessions, and to fit in with his pack's (i.e. your family's) routine. To help him do this, you must teach him Basic Control.

Shape him by modern training methods, reinforcing good behaviour with rewards. *(See Rewards, page 178)*

It is strongly recommended that every dog owner, whether pet or sporting, trains these essential Basic Control exercises.

ESSENTIALS		
ACTION	**COMMAND**	**HINTS**
Name	"Bramble" or whatever	You must both know it. He must stop whatever he is doing and look to you for his next action.
Recall*	**"Come"**	He must return to you instantly.
Positions Stationary	**"Sit"***	Trunk and legs straight, rump on ground, rear legs tucked.
	"Down"*	Body and all feet on ground. An instant Down can be a life saver.
	"Stand"*	
Moving/ Heelwork*	**"Back"*** **"Close"***	Basic position i.e. sit straight by your left leg. Then he moves forward with you.
	"In"*	Go to Indoor Kennel, Car etc.
Staying put & wait*	**"Settle"*** **"Stay"***	The stay put but relaxed. Stay but in whatever position you left him in until you return to him.
	"Wait"*	He stays until you call him to you.
Retrieve*	**"Hold"***	He holds article in his mouth firmly, without chewing, mouthing etc.
	"Give"*	He releases to hand.
Negatives	**"No"*** **"Leave"***	He stops whatever instantly. He drops whatever and/or ignores it.

DESIRABLES		
Basic Position*	**"Watch"**	He looks at you in Basic Position at sit on the move.
Retrieve* Search*	**"Find"**	He looks for hidden or lost articles (then **"Hold"**etc).
Barking*	**"Speak"** **"Quiet"**	We strongly recommend these commands.

* *For training methods, see separate entries.*

BASIC POSITION
The Basic Position element is crucial to much formal training, particularly walking accurately to heel.

Your dog must be to your left, his shoulder close to your leg, ideally parallel with the seam of the trousers. His feet should be virtually parallel, but slightly behind your toes. Your dog should watch you, and, when stationary, he should sit. You must guide your pup into this Basic Position using all the

The Basic Position.

Photo: Steve Nash.

aids: your voice, command "Sit", your hands and the lead to guide him round.

ATTENTION TRAINING
• When your dog has mastered the position in the Sit, command "Watch".
• After initially very short periods, he should be allowed to relax with the command "Off", and be given a reward (praise, treat and/or a game).
• Progressively increase the "Watch" period and the eye contact.
• Eventually use distractions (with your dog being reminded that he is still under "Watch"). Corrected when he inevitably looks away to see what else is happening.
• Progress to "Watch" on the move, on the lead, then off-lead
   Do not build in error. Take your time to perfect this training element.

BEAGLING
See Hounds, page 148.

BEHAVIOUR THERAPY
Behaviour therapy is defined as "treatment of neurotic condition by gradual training to react normally".
Concise Oxford Dictionary.

Behaviourism is a new science although it can be traced from the physiology of Pavlov through other branches of science including anthropology, zoology and psychology to ethology.

A veterinary practice will deal with the dog's physical problems, and, to some extent nervous and mental conditions as well. However, there is now an increasing opportunity for vets to refer problem dogs to a behaviourist, in the same way that a doctor would refer a patient with mental and emotional problems to a psychiatrist or counsellor.

Behaviourist John Rogers described his work as:
• Establishing the root causes of why dogs behave as they do.
• Getting the owner to understand the root cause.
• Designing a behaviour modification programme which will change the behaviour.
• Getting the owner to understand how to apply that programme.

A trainer shapes the behaviour of his dog into taking positive action. But while a trainer would also reshape behaviour by aversion, diversion and other techniques, a behaviourist would endeavour to take away the cause of the behaviour leaving nothing further to shape or reshape.

BEST IN SHOW
This is the highest award a pedigree/purebred dog can win in conformation shows.

In all Breed shows, the winner of each class will compete within its own breed for Best of Breed at that show. The winner of this title will then compete for Best in Group against the Best of Breeds from other breeds within the same Group. The winners of the Best in Group then compete against each other for the title Best in Show. The winner of this title at Crufts will be called 'Supreme Champion' and at Westminster the 'WKC Best in Show'.

BITING
Dogs bite to play, eat and kill. They must be shaped *never* to bite humans.

Dogs are descended from wolves. They have the same efficient teeth and jaws. Wolf packs and dogs in the wild have to kill to live.

Your dog is now in a human pack. As his pack leader, you provide his food and rearing. There is no need for your dog to

Biting is an instinctive form of attack – the well-trained security dog is trained to release on command.

kill or to bite humans *ever*. (Police, Patrol Dog, and Manwork specialists are outside the scope of this book.)

As pack leader you must control all games, including those in which your dog uses his teeth: retrieving, tugging etc. You must win these games and your dog must *never* bite you. Shape him in the following ways:

POSITIVE SHAPING
Start with your puppy. Nature gives him needle-sharp teeth – and they can hurt. When playing, he learns not to bite his littermates nor his mother too hard. Do as she does and give an instant reprimand – shout "Ow!"
Train Basic Control *(see page 91)*, but briefly:
• Use positive "Hold" using a toy, dumbbell etc. A dog cannot bite if his mouth is already full
• Use instant "Down". Again, it is more difficult to bite when lying.

DIVERSION
See page 122, but briefly:
• Watch and learn your dog's body language *(see page 97)*. If his hackles are up, he is stiff-legged, baring his teeth and/or growling, then he may bite next.
• As a puppy divert him by giving him a toy to hold and play games away from the perceived threat.
• When he is older, use Basic Control training to divert him. Get him to "Watch" you, then do Heelwork "Close", "Finish", "Heel", etc.
• Put him to the "Down", a submissive posture.

AVERSION
See page 87, but briefly:
• Hearing: Shout "Ow!". Train the use of the Sound (e.g. tin-can, discs etc.) technique.
• Sight: Use your body language to discipline by frown or scowl or loom.

• Taste: Train the bad taste (e.g. bitter apple) technique.
• Touch: Do as his mother does. An immediate shake coupled with "No!", and frown etc. Use the sudden water-squirt on his face from the detergent bottle/water-pistol.

PREVENTION
If all the above techniques have failed, including the dominance reduction programme (see Aggression, page 75), then you must still protect your family, other humans and your dog:
• Outside: Contain him with a muzzle (webbing or plastic are washable, leather is durable), and a lead.
• Inside: Contain him in his kennel or crate. Put on his muzzle before any visitors enter.
• Physical: With a male, consider neutering. A reduction in dominance usually reduces dominance biting.

RECOMMENDATIONS
• Start shaping your dog from puppyhood.
• Never let him bite you (or any humans including your children whom he may regard as littermates), even in play
• If he does bite, do not reward him for letting go. While this is natural for you, your reward may tempt him to bite again in order to get the reaction of praise/reward.

BOARDING
Boarding kennels vary enormously in quality, and the happiness of your dog, and how well he settles, depends on making the right choice.

While all kennels have to be licensed by their local regulatory authority, requirements are minimum and, indeed, there is little enforcement action taken, even if the minimums are not adhered to.
   Look before you book. An inspection is essential unless you have had a firm recommendation from a trusted friend or colleague. Check the kennelling, check the runs, see how the other dogs look and behave. Speak not just to the owners but also to the kennel staff with regard to feeding, grooming, exercise etc.
   When you leave your dog, a few reminders of home, such as a blanket or toy may be helpful, but do not overdo it. Remember that within two days your dog will have adjusted to his new environment. It is anthropomorphic of us to think

that our dogs are pining for us – they are not. Don't over-apologise before you go, nor on your return. If you must anthropomorphise, assume that your dog is having a holiday and is enjoying a change of scene.

BODY LANGUAGE – Human
Dogs communicate with each other as much by their body language as by sounds. They 'read' bodies – and that includes humans. While some humans are good at noticing if others are happy, sad, pleased, angry etc., dogs are so much better at it, and so we must be aware of the messages we are putting across.

The trained gundog responds to hand signals. Photo: Graham Cox.

A dog may not understand every word you say, but he certainly does understand human displays of emotion. Use this language in your dog's shaping. Show him positively:
• Reward: Smile, look happy when you praise him.
• Aversion: Scowl, frown, loom when you want to deter him.
• Signals: Hand and arm signals are used successfully for deaf dogs. Be aware of the body signals you are giving him when you walk, turn and stop.

It is recommended that you keep a list of your body signals (e.g. hand palm up for 'Stop', extended left for 'Go left', arm and hand for 'Go down', hand front and behind for 'Finish', etc), and ensure that your human pack and instructor use exactly the same signals.

Remember, your head, arms and body say as much as your voice.

BODY LANGUAGE – Dogs
Dogs communicate with each other with body language.

Dogs rely on body language to communicate feelings and intentions.

As pack leader, you must learn to read your dog's language.

Although dogs also communicate vocally by barking (for attention, food, fear, contact), most of their 'talking' is done with their bodies. They posture with their bodies; they indicate with their tails, ears, eyes, eye contact, and facial expressions. As pack leader, you must learn canine body language, and, remember, he will also be reading you! Some points to look for:

FACE
• Ears: pricked = alert, listening; laid back = submission or attack.
• Eyes: half-closed = submission or pleasure; shut = asleep.
• Mouth: lips back, teeth bared = aggression.
VOICE
• Growl real rumbling = aggression; low murmur = pleasure.
• Bark = challenge, warning, communication, fear.
• Howl = distress cry for attention, or long distance communication.
BODY
• Hackles (hairs on back of neck and shoulder) = aggression (but with puppies, sometimes play).
• On toes, head up, chest forward = enlargement, dominance.
• Head down, roll over = submission.
• Front feet forward, head down, bounce = invitation to play.
TAIL
• Wagging = pleasure.
• Stiff, slow wave = aggression.
• Clamped low* = fear.

* Some breeds have their own specific behaviour e.g. Greyhounds and Whippets have natural low tail carriage, and some breeds, notably Retrievers and Dalmatians 'smile' like humans.

You must learn to read your dog and train the other human members of your pack to do so.

BORE
"A person who talks endlessly about his dog's training and behaviour but won't listen when you talk about yours". *Frank Manolson*

BREED SHOWS
Breed shows are essentially beauty competitions for pedigree (purebred) dogs.

A lot of hard work and training goes into preparing a dog for breed showing.
Photo: Carol Ann Johnson.

Anyone contemplating breeding dogs for show purposes should expect to work extremely hard for little reward in order to achieve their goal. The competition is intense, particularly in the more popular breeds where large entries may be expected. Both you and your dog must have the right apptitude and attitude.

The smart appearance of your dog in the ring is of paramount importance. Your dog must be well groomed, with clean feet with hair and nails clipped, plus clean eyes, ears, teeth and nose.

Each breed has its own Breed Standard – a written blueprint of the 'ideal' dog – so you must be confident your dog falls within these parameters before you start your showing career. This will avoid major disappointment later.

Classes are organised into breeds, and then further divided into several age and handicap groups. National Kennel Clubs have details of rules and regulations, and the qualifications needed for a dog to become a Champion. *(See Addresses, page 208; for training, see Ring Training, page 179).*

BRIBERY
Modern dog training is based on behaviour shaping with the use of rewards as reinforcement. Rewards e.g. treats are given immediately for successful behaviour, and simply withheld when the action is not successfully performed.

Some dog trainers, often schooled in earlier methods, claim that this is "bribery", or they say: "I never train my dog with food – that would be bribery".

However, these same people all receive pay for their main occupations which they do not consider "bribery", nor do they consider praise for good results in classes and indeed promotion as bribery. To be fair, when this is pointed out many of the objectors change their views.

A useful example can be taken from Karen Pryor's seminal book *Don't Shoot the Dog* when she describes training dolphins. Training dolphins is more difficult than training dogs, and the aids available are fewer – just fish, back-scratching and noise. Dolphins are just like humans, and come to that, dogs. No reward, no work.

No handler need fear that by using well-timed treats or other rewards correctly that he is having to resort to 'bribery'. Properly used and properly timed rewards are just that, rewards.

C

CANINE FREESTYLE (US), HEELWORK TO MUSIC (UK)
The newest canine activity and sport for trained dogs is working to music.

This activity has grown up in recent years in both the US and the UK. It has developed naturally from the precision dressage element of advanced Obedience, but like ice dancing, it is set to music.

This new discipline has become a demonstration activity (e.g. Heelwork to Music at Crufts and Freestyle Fantasy in the US). It is fascinating to watch and is growing in popularity.

Since 1996 it became a competitive sport in the US and in the UK. In the US, for example, there are now graduated competitions for pairs (handler and dog), at Novice, Intermediate and Advanced level. Marks are awarded as in ballroom dancing or Olympic skating: one for technical merit and one for artistic impression. The judges even hold up cards for each (from 1 to 10).

There are plans for international competition between the US and the UK as soon as the rules are equalised. Video linking, and, after the lifting of UK quarantine, head to head competition is likely and is likely to prove very popular.

CANINE GOOD CITIZEN PROGRAM (US)
See Good Citizens, page 140.

CAR and TRAVEL
Many, possibly now the majority of dog owners, at least in the Western world, own cars. To a dog, the car becomes another home, another den, and often the prelude to an exciting occasion. Many dogs are driven to their walk places daily or even more often. Dogs must be trained to be in and around cars. Indeed, given the lethal nature of a car this is essential and possibly life-saving.

BEFORE DRIVING OFF
Entry: Train your puppy to "Sit" when approaching the rear of the car. Give him his reward, and then, and only then, command him to get into the car "In". Again praise him for so doing.
Exit: Similarly, when you want your pup out of the car, tell him to "Wait" while you open the door. Keep opening and closing the door until he is sitting still and then, but only then, attach the lead and give a release command "Out" or "Off" and reward. Even with adult dogs, it is a good idea to make your dog sit immediately after getting out of the car. This gives a moment of calm before the dog dashes off to investigate or play.
In the car: The use of a crate or a dog guard – a barrier between the dog and driver – is recommended. *See*

The safe way to transport your dog.   Photo: Keith Allison.

Containment, page 114. Practise putting your pup within the
car in his 'place' (his crate or behind the dog guard) before
taking him on a journey. Command "Sit" before you open the
door. Put your dog in the car with the command "In". Reward
him for being there (praise, treat, click etc.), then give him a
chew/toy as you would with the use of a new crate elsewhere.
Train a session or two of this while stationary. Wait until you
are both comfortable before you attempt a short journey.

DRIVING OFF
Some dogs take car travel in their stride, others become hyped
up, (moving around constantly), particularly as the car is
often the prelude to an exciting occasion.
   Over-excitement inside the car can be contained in various
ways:
• Tether your dog to a load point with a yard (metre) long
leash. Ensure that you use an ordinary buckle collar, leather
or webbing. Do not use a choke. This will allow your dog to
lie down, stand up, turn round etc., but will stop him from
charging. It also means you have effective control when you
open the tailgate.
• Use a proprietary dog harness, utilising a seat belt. It has
padding as chest protection and a handle for the lead.
• Use the crate, and if your dog is still excitable while driving,
try putting a cloth over the cage to shut out the view. This
often has a calming effect.

C

CAR SICKNESS

Perseverance is often the best remedy. Behaviourists advise
handlers not to caress a dog when he has been ill, as this may,
in fact, appear to the dog to be a reward for the behaviour of
being ill. Keep the journey short and give rewards when
reaching your destination (a run in the park, games etc.).

There are many effective calming medicines (similar to
those used for humans), both mainstream and homoeopathic,
which can be used. Some may be bought over the counter,
others need to be prescribed by your vet.

FRESH AIR

Dogs should never be confined in stationary cars, unless great
care is taken to ensure they have an adequate supply of fresh
air, and there is no danger of them over-heating. The
temperature inside a car can build up, even on cloudy days.
To ensure safety and security for limited periods of time, the
following measures can be taken:
• Confine the dog in his crate and leave the tailgate open.
• Install a car-vent which fits into the car window.
• Use a lock which fits into the rear lock and catch, leaving a
fixed gap for air which is too small for escape or intrusion.

These measures also prevent a dog from escaping and keep
him secure from intruders.

CAR CHASING

Car chasing is learnt behaviour. It must be discouraged before
it becomes an ingrained habit. *(See Chasing, page 105)*

Dogs that chase for fun can be more easily shaped than
those that are apparently predatory. In the case of the fun-
chaser, his behaviour must be reshaped by diversion *(see page
122)* – giving things other than the chosen targets to chase,
e.g. a favourite toy (a ball on a rope, etc.) when out on a walk.
A fun chaser will prefer to chase a toy as this can be done on
a regular basis.

Other methods to cure chasing are covered by aversion (e.g.
sound, *(see page 87)*, and other diversion therapies. If all else
fails use prevention Containment techniques *(see
Containment, page 114).*

CATS

**There are more cats than dogs in both the USA and in
UK, and many families keep both animals. Co-existence
between dogs and cats is essential for a harmonious**

household. In most cases, a dog's behaviour needs to be shaped appropriately.

The cartoon chase of dog after cat is legendary. Dogs chase cats because they are programmed to chase. Cats run because this is their first line of defence. If a cat is cornered and turns on its attacker, clawing across the attacker's nose, the dog will usually back off and the cat will escape. Speed and precision will win the day, and in most cases, the cat will inflict most damage.

In order to avoid such skirmishes, which can become dangerous, the dog must learn to live alongside the cat (or cats) in his house and the instinct to chase must be subdued.

SUPERVISED INTRODUCTION
Introduce the puppy to the cat. When introducing the puppy to an adult cat, restrain the puppy – not the cat. If the cat stands its ground it will probably show signs of aggression, hissing or spitting, with fur raised, and the puppy will back off. If the cat runs away from the puppy be ready to distract the puppy so that he does not give chase. Continue to restrain the puppy until the cat is accustomed to his presence, and the puppy has learnt that the cat is not for chasing.

A puppy will soon learn to respect a cat.

Photo: Steve Nash.

CHASING AND PLAY
Use standard techniques
• Aversion *(page 87)* e.g. Water squirt, sound, etc. to reinforce the 'no chase' behaviour. Don't forget to reward for good behaviour.

• Diversion *(page 122)*

As a puppy grows he may try to make the cats play with him. When you see this happening, you must again use diversion techniques to ensure that the puppy plays with the human pack leader who must be the source – preferably the only source – of games.

CHAIN/CHECK CHAIN
See Collars, page 110.

CHASING
You must shape your dog not to chase anything or anybody (except on command only, in some specific service activities and some sports).

'Anything' includes cars, vehicles generally, and bicycles. 'Anybody' means anybody, but particularly runners, joggers, cats etc. Chasing is not only anti-social it is also inherently dangerous to dog and human.

Dogs like a chase. Moreover if the dog is on his own territory and the car, bicycle etc. is nearby, the dog is self-rewarded. The dog chases. The car disappears. The dog has 'won'. He has successfully defended his territory – and had a good game in the process.

TRAINING TECHNIQUES
Train your dog as a puppy, or as soon as he comes into your pack. Use the standard techniques:

POSITIVE TRAINING
Basic Control: Recall (Name, "Come"); Positions ("Down"), Heelwork ("Close"). A dog cannot chase if he is with you, under your control.
Diversion: Play a game. Get your dog to retrieve and "Hold" – he cannot chase as well.

NEGATIVE TRAINING
Aversion: Use the sound techniques (can, rattle, discs); touch techniqes (e.g. set up a sting with hose or water-filled balloons which can be fired from a friend's car, bicycle etc.
Prevention: Confine your dog in the house or in his kennel, or on a long lead in the garden/yard. Consider consulting an animal behaviourist. *(See Containment, page 114).*

CHEWING
This is entirely natural and is common to all puppies. It is important to recognise the need, and to ensure that it is catered for effectively.

It is natural for a puppy to chew, but you can ensure that this habit is kept in reasonable check.

All puppies will chew at some time. They go through various phases. The first is when they are small and learning to use their mouths. The second is when they are acquiring their adult teeth, usually between the ages of four and six months.

There is a third phase when a growing puppy is large enough to be interested in prey, but not yet skilled in catching it. In the wild, the pack leader will bring back large chunks of food for the youngsters to chew. When a pack leader, or superior beings in the pack, leave things lying around, it is perfectly natural for puppies to look on such articles as welcome gifts.

Translated into a domestic set-up, these 'gifts' include slippers, shoes, gloves – with their 'pack leader's' splendid scent on them – as well as offerings from their 'littermates' (the children) which include an exciting variety of toys.

While we therefore understand a puppy's need to chew in order to deal with teething problems, and to explore their world through a process of self-education, it is nevertheless important for us humans to teach the dogs in our pack what they are allowed to chew and what is forbidden.

In addition to his normal food ration, give the pup aids to chew to help him through the teething process. These include hard rubber toys, hide chews, and marrow bones, given under supervision.

Train your puppy not to chew the pack leader's possessions. Use the following techniques:-

POSITIVE TRAINING
Diversion: Remove the article from the pup with a firm "No", and, as a diversion, substitute one of the pup's own chew toys with the command "Chew". The "Hold" command can be taught after the puppy has finished teething. *(see Diversion, page 122)*

NEGATIVE TRAINING
Aversion: When the pup is seen to be chewing, shape his behaviour by sound (e.g. discs ; touch, e.g. squirting with water *(see Aversion, page 87)*. Many people have also had success using the smell/taste technique (e.g. a bitter apple spray or similar proprietary liquids that are available) on furniture and other articles that have already been chewed, or may be vulnerable to chewing. The smell and taste is very unpleasant to a dog, and will put a stop to any wish to chew.
Prevention: Never leave a pup to run round the house when you are out or when you are busy. Use the crate, or confine the puppy in an area where there is nothing of value that he can chew. Remember, it will be too late to correct him for chewing when you return.

CHILDREN
Children and dogs can and do give each other great happiness. As the young are, however, unpredictable at times in their behaviour, both must be supervised by responsible adult handlers.

THE DO'S
• Socialise your puppy with children and other dogs. Equally, socialise your children with dogs.
• Supervise games and beware of over-excitement both during roll-around games and at feeding times.
• "Control the games and you control the dog". *(John Rogerson)*.

Remember that puppies and dogs bite. They do this particularly when they are excited, and puppies when playing often give each other a nasty nip causing a squeal. Beware of this happening to children. The dog is a pack animal and needs to know his place in the hierarchy. Ensure, therefore, that your dog does not assume that he holds higher ranking than your children merely because he regards them as littermates.

Teach your puppy Basic Control *(see page 91)*, then train your children to use exactly the same words, and, if possible, the same tone that you yourself use. Allow your children to add treats to your puppy's bowl while he is eating. In this way, your pup will not see a child's approach to his bowl as a threat. This will also reinforce the ranking in the hierarchy with the child as superior to the dog.

THE DON'TS
• Do not give an untrained child a puppy to train.
• Do not allow biting. Although natural to a puppy and part of his play with littermates, you must stop a puppy nipping or biting children or other humans.

CLICKER TRAINING
A clicker is a comparatively new tool in the dog trainer's armoury. It is based on the Pavlovian principle of conditioning a dog's reflexes to a specific noise.

The clicker itself is a simple and inexpensive device. It consists of a plastic box (2 inches x 1 inch or 5 cm x 2.5 cm) which has a hole in the top, in the middle of which is a metal tongue. By pressing the tongue through the hole in the top and releasing it, a click results. Its use is for positive reinforcement of conditioned behaviour shaping. It is one of the "two horns of the same goat" with sound aversion *(see page 87)*. As the sound of the discs is used to reduce unwanted behaviour, so the clicker sound is used to reinforce wanted behaviour.

Above: A simple device, clicker-training is based on association.

Right: The dog soon learns that the sound of the clicker signals a treat.

Amazing results have been obtained by dog trainers using clickers as an adjunct to the other rewards and shaping methods. Dogs for the Disabled are currently using clicker training with considerable success. It was used to great effect not only to train dogs, but young pigs for the film *Babe*. Because pigs mature at such a speed, a series of pigs were needed (to have one at the same age through the process of filming). Over 200 pigs were trained for this one film using clicker methods.

CONSISTENCY AND TIMING

To be effective, the device must be used with consistency and with good timing. The principle is Pavlovian: click when the pup or dog being trained does the action to be desired, and withhold the click when it does not.

There are now books, videos and indeed courses demonstrating this method. It is important for interested handlers to see a demonstration, and to get as much information as possible before starting. Good instruction is vital. As with so many training methods, wrong use, and particularly wrong timing, can do considerable harm.

Do not use both the clicker and sound aversion at the same time. The clicker gives positive reinforcement and the discs give negative reinforcement. Unless the handler is very skilled, use of both is likely to cause confusion.

This is an exciting new technique. Do give it consideration for your next puppy.

CLOTHING
Clothing for dog training must be appropriate.

This is obvious for the more rugged outside walking and training, and for sports (e.g. shooting/hunting, Field Trials, Beagling, Working Trials etc.).

It is surprising how often new handlers come for training, or even for dog walking, wearing inappropriate footwear and clothing. High heels, fashion boots, flip-flops etc. are simply not suitable for heelwork or indeed other dog activities. They are a potential danger to the handler and give no help to the dog. Trainers/sneakers are ideal for indoor and smooth surface training outdoors. There are specialist shoes available for precision Obedience, Agility etc. and, of course, waterproof boots for walking, shooting, Trials etc.

With the exception of breed showing, handlers, both men and women, should preferably wear trousers; a skirt will flap in the dog's face and stop him watching the handler. Care should also be taken to see that jackets and top garments do not flap in the dog's face. Try to remember to have garments with pockets for the aids and, in particular, for rewards. Given the need to give a treat, to click etc. *instantaneously*, the garments should not only have pockets but swift easy access to them.
Give the dog a chance – wear appropriate footwear and clothing!

CLUBS
It is highly desirable that all dog owners should join a good training club as soon as possible.

A club will help with basic training and socialisation with other dogs and with people. Details of clubs in your area can be obtained from your national Kennel Club, your local library, your vet or the specialist magazines.

If you intend to go further with training and try competition, the club will be able to guide you. As with all sports, the sooner you and, indeed, your dog start, the better. It is vital for you both to be set off on the correct path.

The first club you join will inevitably be Obedience and/or Breed Ring training. This is because there are few sporting clubs (e.g. Working Trials or Agility) that offer classes in control since it is not possible to compete in such sports before a pup is eighteen months old or more when its bones have set.

In addition to training at a club, you may do well by self-training. Each of the sports and activities now has excellent books with pictures and diagrams; most also have videos. At the top level, as with many other sports, competitors make use of a private trainer.

If you want to compete, check whether the club has a competition section. Local clubs often have internal competitions where pups move from a junior class up to a senior class and may also have inter-club matches.

Ask fellow handlers or your vet for recommendations. Visit the club without your dog. See if their methods (fun-shaping by reward and not shout, yank and smack compulsion by punishment) are what you want.

Look before you book.

COLLARS

All dogs must wear a collar with a name tag both as legal and practical requirements. But which? There is a bewildering choice available with a range of material, design and fastenings. Some are more suitable for particular types of training than others.

THE CHOICE

Material: Includes leather, nylon or cotton webbing, chain (steel), plastic, even iron is available.

Design: Fixed circle; slip; halter; figure of eight; choke/check; half-check.

Fastening: Buckle, spring-clip, pistol release, small chain link for the half-check. Slip (for quick release for sporting dogs etc.).

Choosing the right collar for your dog depends on breed (head, carriage and neck), and what you are trying to accomplish. A pet needs a different collar from those in specific occupations or sports. The range of collars include:

• FULL BUCKLE: This is still the most popular collar for pet dogs. Design is a matter of personal choice.

• HALF-CHECKS: These are made of leather or nylon webbing (washable for hygiene) which are expandable, and they are ideal for training. A small loop of chain is fastened between two D-rings. As the collar is fitted so that the leather/webbing is only around the neck of the dog, when the chain is flicked the collar merely reaches round the dog's neck without undue pressure. It cannot choke the dog, cut off his wind supply, or harm him in any other way.

A rapid flick and release also stops the dog pulling. The principle is akin to that of light hands on a horse's rein.

• CHOKE CHAINS: Although these are still used by many of the security forces for training their dogs, modern trainers have moved on from the use of full chokes since they are difficult to use for beginners and unnecessary for experienced handlers.

• ANTI-PULL: There are a number of anti-pull designs, some patented. Examples are the harness, figure of eight, halter. The Halti, Col-leash, Dogalter, and the Gentle Leader.

• THERAPEUTIC: There are collars which can be used therapeutically. For example, one with a magnet in it is used against arthritis; another is copper against rheumatism.

• COMPUTERISED: There is a collar which has in it a tiny computer. This, when coupled with the remainder of the equipment – an antenna wire buried on the outside edge of the property and a transmitter – trains the dog to stay within the chosen site. *(See Containment, page 114)*

The Gentle Leader.
Photo courtesy: Dogs Today.

The Dogalter.
Photo courtesy: Dogs Today.

THE LAW
Under current law in the UK and in most of the US, every dog on a highway or in a public place must wear a collar with the name and address of his owner inscribed on it or on a plate or badge attached to it. A highway includes any road or footpath over which the public have the right to pass.

Collars are not required for dogs being used for sporting purposes, for the capture or destruction of vermin, for the driving or tending of cattle or sheep, for any dog being used by the Services or the Police in emergency rescue work, and for dogs registered with the Guide Dog for the Blind Association or Seeing Eye.

In all other instances, if your dog does not have a collar he may be taken by the Police or the dog warden and be treated as a stray. In the UK, you will be guilty of an offence and may be prosecuted and fined.

COLLAR TRAINING

As soon as you arrive home with your pup, put a lightweight collar on him so that he can become used to it. Do not attach the lead to begin with but simply leave the collar round his neck quite loosely. He may fight this for some time by scratching at it and rolling. You should ignore this behaviour, but reward (praise, clicker, treat etc.) as soon as he stops. *See Lead, Leash, Lead-training page 157.*

COME

See Basic Control page 91: Recall page 171.

COMMANDS
Your dog must obey each single command, instantly.

Do not give repeated commands, allowing your dog to respond in his own time, if at all. This delay is an example of dominance *(see page 125)*.

Basic Control is essential. Join an obedience club and/or obtain books and videos on training. Join the appropriate KC Good Citizen Dog Scheme/AKC Good Citizen Program *(see Good Citizens page 140)*

In all stages of training, it is very important that you always use the *same*, single words of command, praise, etc. and the same *tone of* voice. Dogs learn by repetition, and so if your commands are different you will cause great confusion and accomplish very little.

If properly taught, your dog will wish to respond to you his pack leader. When a command is correctly carried out, reinforce by reward (by praise, a treat, the clicker, a favourite toy and/or a game). Constant use of the command using all the aids (voice, lead, hands, a click, reward) will shape correct behaviour.

Always use the dog's name to get his attention, then give the single word command. See Vocabulary *(page 201)* for words and signals, and Basic Control *(page 91)* for training.

Keep a list of your commands, whether voice, signal, whistle, etc. Ensure all your human pack (and your instructor) use exactly the same commands.

COMPETITIONS
See Sports page 189.

COMPULSION
This is the 'act of compelling', i.e. using force to attain an objective.

Many dog trainers used to, and a few still do, try compulsion. Yank his lead, scream at him, beat him. Compulsion as a training technique has never been very successful whether with children, dogs, or employees. The only lesson actually learnt is to avoid the compeller.

We no longer teach children or employees by force, and it has been found that we cannot train dolphins or most other animals with force.

Thankfully, training dogs is now on a par with other education and training, and we now encourage ('shape') our dog to act positively and then reinforce him for a reward (e.g. praise, treat, game, clicker etc.) so that he does the exercise/action because he is happy to, rather than because he has been forced to, by out-dated compulsion and punishment.

CONTAINMENT
Dog training is divided into four parts: the two positives of shaping and reinforcement through rewards, and diversion – and the two negatives of aversion, and prevention. Containment, which is vital for the safety and security of dogs as well as people, is the cornerstone of preventative training.

Containment can be divided into four areas: Indoors, Outdoors – but within the owner's property, Car or other enclosed vehicle, Outdoor – outside the owner's property.

INDOORS
Crate: The use of an indoor crate is invaluable. It gives a puppy security, separates it from other members of the pack (including small children etc.) gives emotional security as his own den equivalent. *(See Crate training page 117)*
Stairgate: This can be used between rooms (to reduce

separation anxiety, *see page 83)* and at the bottom of stairs.
The gate allows superior members of the pack, i.e. the
humans, to pass through but prevents the dog from following.
Doors: Use internal doors to separate the house into various
territories. Dogs must be trained to accept that they do not
have access to all their owner's territory and may be
contained, for example, in the kitchen.
House Line: This is a line, measuring 6-9 ft, which is
attached to an ordinary collar with buckle and D-ring. It
enables the owner to stop the pup doing whatever is devious.
Using it does require skill, and many find that it gets tangled
and will then be counter-productive.

OUTDOORS – OWN PROPERTY
Kennel: The use of an outdoor kennel and run is a solution
adopted by many. Kennels must be weatherproof, well-
drained, and shaded.
Tether: This may be a line of chain or leather (provided the
dog is not a chewer) securely anchored to an immovable
object, and attached to the dog's collar with buckle and D-
ring. It may be used within a kennel and run.
Fencing: It is possible to 'dog proof' your own back garden
or yard by adequate, secure fencing. It must be high enough
so that the dog will not jump over it, and sufficiently dense so
that the dog will not dig or eat his way through.
Electric Wire Fence: Electric wire fencing, as used for the
containment of sheep, horses and other livestock, is not
adequate for dogs. Dogs can jump or burrow more easily than
the other animals and it is seldom secure.
Electronic Fencing: This is a system that has been improved
in recent years. The principle is that a transmitter wire is
buried around the perimeter of the space where the dog is to
be contained. If the wire is twisted it is inert, so, as well as
creating a boundary, it can be used to go round other sensitive
areas, for example, swimming pools, flower beds, play areas.

   The dog is fitted with a collar that has a small microchip
computer within it. The perimeter wire is wired to an electric
transformer with battery back-up. The principle is that the
wire gives a signal to the collar which, initially induces a mild
electric shock. The dog has to be trained in the use of the
collar, although this is simply done by standard aversion *(see
page 87)* and diversion *(see page 122)* techniques.

CARS AND VEHICLES
For the protection of both dog and driver, it is recommended that you use one of the following:
Dog guard: This is fitted in the rear of the vehicle.
Specialist cage: These can be fitted inside the car. The indoor crate can also be used for this purpose.
Tether or harness: These are fitted to the interior of the car.
(See Car and Travel page 101)

OUTDOORS – OUTSIDE PROPERTY
Every dog must wear a collar, and carry some form of identification. For outdoor work a lead is also an essential. It is important to train your dog to walk on a lead without pulling. *(See Lead training, pages 157).* For those experiencing problems, there are a number of anti-pulling devices available. *(See Collars, page 111).*

If you want to leave your dog outside a shop for a short period of time, ensure that the restraint is fixed at your dog's end to the D-ring in a buckle collar, and not to a choke or slip collar. There are portable tethers with points which screw into the earth. Test stability and safety before leaving your dog on his own.

CONTROL
See Basic Control page 91.

CRABBING
Crabbing is a term used in the sport of Obedience to describe a dog who is not in the correct basic position.

The correct position in heelwork is for the dog's shoulders to be close to his handler's leg and at right angles to his handler. A crabbing dog walks forward with his lead leg, the nearside off, leading, so that the dog's head is around and often impeding the handler's left leg. This, in turn, makes the dog's hindquarters project at an angle outwards away from the handler.

RETRAINING
Crabbing can be cured by retraining with the Basic Position *(page 92)*, and on lead *(page 157)*.

The old school of training advocated the use of a body leash (a second lead round under the dog's abdomen with the lead behind the handler). The handler, with his right hand, can

With a little encouragement, a puppy will soon feel at home in his crate.

Photo: Keith Allison.

then pull the dog back and straight. Modern methods rely on the positive rewards to shape the desired behaviour, i.e. a straight position.

CRATE TRAINING
An indoor crate/kennel is an invaluable aid to training during puppyhood, and it can be put to many uses for the adult dog.

FUNCTIONS
A crate can be used for the following:
• Ensuring that your home remains in one piece if you have to leave your puppy at home when the chewing stages start.
• Separating your puppy from children and other playmates (for rest, feeding, etc.)
• Separating your puppy when visitors arrive.
• Teaching your puppy to travel in a car and when staying away from home.
• As an aid to house-training *(see page 149)*

TRAINING TECHNIQUES
Shape your puppy to use the crate as soon as you get him home. Use his name and rattle his food dish. Put his food dish in the crate and let him eat there. Later use treats, the clicker, or a favourite toy or a chew. Command "Settle"each time you put him in his crate. He will soon learn that the cage/crate is his territory and associate it with relaxation.
    It is recommended that:-
• You do not allow children or visitors to fuss the dog inside his crate. Take him out first.
• You move his crate from place to place. This is a prelude to

using a cage/crate for travelling.
See Car and Travel page 101; Containment page 114)

CRUFTS
The UK Kennel Club describes Crufts with total lack of modesty but with total accuracy as 'The World's Greatest Dog Show'. It brings the "best of the very best in all that is positive about dogs".

Crufts is held at the National Exhibition Centre in Birmingham, situated in the centre of England. The show runs for four days, usually in March each year. It covers a number of disparate activities all dealing with dogs. Among the best known are the Supreme Championship during which some 20,000 top pedigree dogs compete for the most prestigious trophy in the world of dogs. Each Group – Gundog, Working and Pastoral, Terrier and Hound, Toys and Utility – is allocated one of the four days. All entries are judged culminating in a Grand Final on the Sunday evening.

In addition to the breed competitions, there are a huge number of other activities relating to dog training, behaviour and care. The Obedience finals is a highspot. During the year Obedience shows are held at various locations, and the winners receive a certificate, known to competitors as a 'ticket', to enter the Obedience finals. The finals are split into dogs and bitches, and there is a competition between each of the two winners to establish the Supreme Obedience Champion.

There is also an Agility Final and a Flyball Final – both fast and furious. Other sports include the Kennel Club Junior Organisation (KCJO) competitions for youngsters aged between eight and eighteen, which are run as both individual and team events.

Crufts also features numerous displays and demonstrations of trained dogs and of dog training too. Demonstrations include many of the activities included in the competitions, such as basic Obedience, Agility, Heelwork to Music, Field Trials, Retrieving and others.

Service dogs are well represented with demonstrations by Police dogs and Sniffer dogs detecting drugs and explosives. Assistance dogs including Dogs for the Disabled, Hearing Dogs for the Deaf, Guide Dogs for the Blind etc., are also featured.

DANGEROUS DOGS

THE LAW IN THE UK

The Dangerous Dogs Act was introduced in 1991. It was politicians' gut reaction to some headline news cases relating specifically to Pit Bull Terriers. Unfortunately, it has gone much further than was ever intended. The Act deals both with dogs bred for fighting (Pit Bulls etc.) which are outside the scope of this book, but also deals with dogs which are 'out of control'. This is relevant to every UK dog owner.

The Act states that "if a dog is dangerously out of control in a public place – (a) the owner and (b) if different the person for the time being in charge of the dog is guilty of an offence, or, if the dog whilst so out of control injures any person, an aggravated offence".

An Order may carry potential terms of imprisonment for the owner/keeper. It may specify the measures to be taken for keeping the dog under proper control whether by muzzling, keeping on a lead or excluding it from specified places or otherwise, and may also require a male dog to be castrated. In the case of an aggravated offence (i.e., one in which actual injury is caused), the Court must make a Destruction Order.

For the purposes of the Act, whether a dog is dangerously out of control or whether there are grounds for reasonable apprehension that it will injure a person, is a question of interpretation at the time. An example was 'Woofie', a dog whose crime was to chase a postman, corner him and bark at him. The dog never actually bit the postman, but nevertheless a Destruction Order was made. Thankfully, the Order was lifted on appeal, but it must be clear to any dog owner that as the law stands currently, there is no excuse ever for a dog to bite. We must train our dogs *never* to use their teeth except when commanded to do so.

THE LAW IN THE USA

The American Kennel Club favours the adoption of reasonable, enforceable, non-discriminatory laws to govern the ownership of dogs. However, while the AKC believes that dog owners should be responsible for their dogs, the American courts have overturned laws that purport to apply only to individual breeds or breed types. Instead, it submits that laws should impose appropriate penalties on irresponsible owners and establish a procedure for dealing with dangerous dogs including, if necessary, the destruction of that dog.

State legislation must foster the safety and protection of the general public from specific animals classified as dangerous or undesirable.

DEN
A dog is a den animal, and despite thousands of years of domestication, the security provided by a den is of paramount importance.

Most pets create their own dens, whether an area has been allocated to them or not. A dog may choose to lie under a particular table or behind a sofa, and this becomes his preferred spot where he feels safe and secure.

You must be aware of this behaviour and shape it by providing the dog with his own 'den' and placing his bed there. If he is to spend all night in the kitchen, for example, then this is obviously the place to allocate as his den.

Use an indoor crate during your puppy's early training. *(See Crate training page 117).* It is of immense benefit for house training, for confining your puppy during the inevitable chewing and destructive behaviour following teething, and for separation from visitors and children.

• Ensure that your dog's den is not a 'no-go' area for you. Stand in it, move it, whatever.

• Do not anthropomorphise. A den, including an indoor crate, means safety and security to a dog. It does not mean a prison.

DEPORTMENT
This is a book about dog training, yet, dog and handler work as a team. If you are all hands and legs in the wrong places you give wrong signals to your dog. Every handler should and every competitor must learn deportment (in competition, handler faults and extra commands are marked, whether or not they are intentional).

It is recommended that you practise deportment without your dog so that he is not thrown wide or out of position by incorrect handling. As always, incorrect teaching reinforces error and is doubly difficult to solve since it has to be unlearned before the correct teaching can be given.

WHAT TO DO
Even though deportment without a dog will raise eyebrows (particularly for us large six-foot tall men!), you should start without your dog.
• Stand with your body relaxed, with the weight from the shoulders over the backside over your heels.
• Move forward with your left hand still, elbow into side. Move off with the left foot, swinging the right arm as balance. Endeavour to practise where there is already a white line or other straight edge which will act as a guide.
• When you have mastered a straight line, then try the turns. Execute these with knees and feet together. Your whole upper trunk, including your head, must move in unison on these turns. To have your shoulders backwards or forwards or your head at an awkward angle will only cause complications and do untold damage to your pup's training.
• When you have mastered normal pace, practise slow pace, then fast.
• Only when you are proficient yourself should you try Heelwork with your dog!

DISCS
See Aversion page 87.

DISTANT CONTROL
Modern teaching theory advises training distant control 'DC' as a puppy. At one time DC was left until the dog was approaching the higher Obedience classes because it is only tested there. However, the change has been made because DC provides training 'elements' for many other exercises. For example, "Down" at a distance can be a life saver for your dog (when approaching traffic, or other potentially dangerous situations.)

THE POSITIONS
There are three DC positions with movements to and from each:
• The Sit, and from there the Down or the Stand.
• The Stand to the Down or the Sit.
• The Down to the Sit or the Stand.

The dog must respond to Sit, Stand and Down in Distant Control.

Photo: Steve Nash.

In Obedience competition the dog has to adopt six positions as directed by the judge.

Train each element as shown under Sit *(page 186)*, Down *(page 128)* Stand *(page 190)*. Only when your dog is proficient at each should you link them together. Start close to the dog. Then extend the distance gradually.

DIVERSION
Diversion is simply training a behaviour which is incompatible with an unwanted action. It is positive shaping, and is one of the four major training techniques. These are the two positives of shaping by reward and reinforcement, and diversion, the negative of aversion and the neutral of containment.

TRAINING TECHNIQUES
It is recommended that you always try positive shaping by reward and reinforcement first. However, diversion is a useful technique.

Use your training to get action, and don't forget the reward (a game, treat etc.) – the "offer he cannot refuse". Training each action/position mentioned is Basic Control. They are covered as "Close" *(Basic Position page 91)*, "Hold" *(Retrieve page 175)*, "Come" *(Recall page 171)*, "Sit" *(page 186)*, "Down" *(page 128)*

Diversion is a commonsense technique. Use it !

Unwanted action	Train Incompatible	Hints
Barking	"Down"	It is difficult for a dog to bark while lying down.
	"Hold"	While holding an article properly he cannot bark as well.
	"Hold" and "Down" together	Even better.
Pulling	"Come"	Recall to you and sit in the present position. Sit in the Basic Position then walk forward with formal Heelwork.
	"Close"	When in the Basic Position at Sit and walking to heel he is not pulling.
Jumping	"Sit"	Close to you.
	"Down"	At a distance. Obviously while he is in the Sit or Down he is not jumping up.
Aggression/ Confrontation	"Come"	When you have recalled him to you he is away from confrontation. You can control him further if needs be e.g. Down.
	Prevention	Containment with lead on etc.
Licking	"Sit" or "Down"	He cannot lick if he cannot reach.
	"Hold"	He cannot lick if his mouth is full.

DOGS FOR THE DISABLED

A relatively recent programme, now rapidly gaining ground, which gives physically disabled owners an increasing degree of mobility and independence.

A variety of different breeds are being used to help owners, often in wheelchairs. Golden Retrievers and Labrador Retrievers are currently among the most successful.

The tasks that a trained dog undertakes are numerous and include:

• Retrieving dropped articles.
• Retrieving incoming mail and newspapers.
• Retrieving items delivered to the door.
• Retrieving a cordless telephone.
• Collecting articles on a shopping expedition.
• Turning lights on and off.
• Barking to raise an alarm.
• Acting as a steadier.

Dogs for the Disabled are trained to carry out a wide variety of tasks.

Following a period of Basic Control training and socialisation, the dog is taught specific tasks using a clicker/reward system. The dog is then matched to a disabled owner, and further specialist training takes place which is specific to the owner's individual needs.

DOG SITTERS
This can be allied to house sitting, and is a variant of putting your dog in a boarding kennel.

The dog sitter, perhaps a relative, perhaps a friend, or very possibly a representative of a company or a free-lance individual will 'sit' your house and your dog.

The perceived advantage of this is to have someone looking after your home, and causing less disruption to your dog when you go away. Ensure you take up references, and be especially careful to check that the handling of your dog is what you expect and require.

DOG WALKERS
In today's increasingly busy age it is not always possible for the owner or handler to give his dog the exercise that is required. One solution to this is employ a dog walker.

This is simply an arrangement between two people when the dog walker will be paid to take the owner's dog for a walk.

Again, the recommendation is the same as with boarding kennels – *look before you book.* As there is no scheme for approving dog walkers, you need to see clear evidence of the dog walker's skills in handling dogs in general and yours in particular. It is also important to ask the following questions:
• How many dogs will be walked at the same time?
• Where are the dogs to be walked?
• Will they be on the lead or allowed free exercise?
• How long will the walk be?

D

DOMINANCE

Some dogs naturally are more dominant than others. Unless the behaviour of excessively dominant dogs is reshaped, they will become a danger to their owners, to other humans, to other dogs – and eventually to themselves.

The dog is a pack animal. Each pack has its own hierarchy. Each rank within the hierarchy has its own privileges. At the head of each pack is a pack leader. The pack leader has more privileges than others in the pack and, in the wild, he also has responsibilities for providing food, shelter, maintaining order, and for the general welfare of the pack.

In a domestic situation these responsibilities are taken away from dogs. However, many dogs are given privileges of rank that they would not receive within their own pack in the wild. The result of this is that the dog perceives that his position is greater than, in fact, it is or should be. This is potentially a very dangerous situation as the dominant dog has all the weapons of its wild ancestors – namely teeth and claws.

It is imperative that the owner realises what is going on, and is prepared to reshape dominant characteristics so that the dog is able to fit into his human pack, and be subordinate to his pack leader.

DOMINANT TRAITS

Dominant traits in dogs show up in many ways:
- Biting – including snarling, nipping, raised hackles etc.
- Doors – charging through doors first.
- Stairs – dashing up stairs, insisting on going first.
- Territory – taking control of part of the house or garden/yard – and then guarding it from intruders. At worst, this can mean that the owner dare not approach. This type of behaviour can also be seen on stairs if the dog is on a higher level than the human members of the family. In this instance, he will take up an aggressive posture and keep the human at bay.
- Furniture – sits or sleeps in a particular chair or sofa, and then guards it.
- Bed – the dog will protect his bed as his own territory. He may appropriate a human's bed.
- Toys – regarded as the dog's exclusive property.
- Games – winning the toy and refusing to give it up.
- Begging – for food and other favours.
- Attention Seeking Devices – nudges, lingering stares into

human eyes, nibbling, holding on to a sleeve, arm, etc. with his mouth.
• Grooming – refuses to have his underparts touched.
• Walks – the dog appears to be leading his owner. When off lead, it will take a number of commands for him to return, if he does so at all.

RESHAPING BEHAVIOUR
The most obvious recommendation is not to allow this type of behaviour to develop. You must assert yourself as pack leader right from the start with your puppy. Ensure that he recognises all human members of his pack as superior in rank to any dog. Use Basic Control *(see pages 91)*

If, however, you are faced with a situation where some or all of the above characteristics are now apparent in your dog, then don't despair. The dog's behaviour can be reshaped with a dominance reduction programme:
BITING: This must never be allowed. See Biting *(page 94)* but, briefly use:
Positive shaping and diversion
• Train "Hold. The dog, annot bite if his mouth is full.
• Train instant "Down". It is more difficult to bite while lying down.
Aversion
• Voice – a sharp "No".
• Taste. Use a repellent, e.g. bitter apple.
Prevention
• Consider castration.
DOORS/STAIRS: The dog must be taught to come second through doors, when going upstairs, or going through gateways and passages.

There are various techniques for this, starting with the most basic of shutting the door on the dog's face. He soon learns. Another technique is to:
• Put the dog on a lead, allow the dog through the door, shut

Behaviour must be reshaped so the dominant dog learns to accept the pack leader's authority.

Photo: Steve Nash.

the door with the dog (still on the lead) on one side and the owner on the other.
• The dog will soon want to go back to see what has happened to the rest of 'his pack'.
• At that point, repeat the procedure until the dog learns that he has to go in or out of the door in second place.

TERRITORY: Reshape your dog so there are no 'no-go' areas in the house or garden. Use:
• The standard aversion techniques of sound e.g. tin can or discs, and taste e.g. bitter apple *(see page 87)* . This will soon persuade the dog that all territory is the owner's, and not his.
• Teach your dog not to lie across doorways, passages, etc. The simple, old-fashioned method is to walk through, not over, nor round, him. Do not apologise. He, not you, must move.

FURNITURE/BED: Do not let your dog claim furniture, chairs, etc. as his own. Use prevention techniques:
• A staircase.
• Shut the door on the room with the desired furniture.
• The crate. *(See Crate-training, page 117)*
   You are the pack leader and own all your territory – he is not, and does not.

BEGGING/ATTENTION SEEKING: This is not so much a sign of devotion, but more a case of the dog shaping you to give food or attention. When you realise this, it is easier for you to reshape the dog by ignoring his heart-rending pleas. Reward him when he does not beg or nudge – never when he does.

GROOMING: You (and the vet) must be able to inspect and groom your dog for his own health and safety. Use the standard techniques:
Basic Control: *See page 91,* but briefly
• Train your dog in the positions "Sit," "Stand", "Down".
• Train him to "Wait" or "Stay".
Containment: *See page 114,* but briefly
• Use the collar and lead, and a muzzle if necessary.
Diversion: *See page 122,* but briefly
• Teach your dog to "Hold" a toy chew, etc.
Aversion: *See page 87,* but briefly
• Use Sound (tin cans, discs, etc.)
TOYS/GAMES: You must win games with a dominant dog.
• Do not allow the dog to take away the toy as a 'trophy'; he must be induced to give it to the handler *(see Retrieve, page 175 and Reward, page 178).*

• As pack leader, you must start the games and stop them, preferably before the dog is bored, and must retain the toy yourself.

WALKS: Shape the dominant dog to stay within the car and house until you let him out. Train your dog to "Sit" and "Wait" until his lead is attached, and then open the door. Train him not to pull on the lead. *(See Pulling page 168)*, but briefly
• Use diversion (producing a toy or initiating a game).
• Change direction (the owner about turns and goes off at an oblique angle) which leaves the dog 'stranded' and having to follow.
• Let the dog charge ahead, and then be pulled up short by the lead (the action and reaction principle). Try one of the purpose-made anti-pull devices available *(see Collars page 111)*.

Remember to continue Basic Control training. Your daily five-minute refresher will give each of you pleasure, and will remind each of you of your position in the pack.

DOWN

Down is an essential command for all dog owners. It is, of course, the position where the dog has his body, and his legs, touching the ground. A swift response to a single word is essential for your dog's safety as well as for others.

The Down position also places the dog in a submissive position, and can therefore be used to defuse any problems between dogs, or between dog and human. Obedience to the Down command at a distance can be a lifesaver when a dog is close to traffic, or livestock.

TRAINING TECHNIQUES
Start training your puppy to obey this command as soon as he is introduced to the household. There are two methods currently in use:

Method I
• Kneel by the puppy when he is standing. Stroke his head from the muzzle backwards until he is relaxed, and then place your thumbs in the hollow between the breast bone and shoulders, with the hands around the shoulders.
• Give the command "Down", and with a firm downwards movement, guide the puppy backwards into the Down position.

A treat is used to guide the puppy into the Down position.

• Reward (praise, treat, etc.) and shortly afterwards give a release command – "Off" or "OK".

Method II

The second method is similar but uses a treat, and most people find it easier.

• Kneel close to the standing dog with a treat at the ready. Show it to your puppy, and then lower it between his front feet and slightly under his chest.

• Give the command "Down", and the puppy will have to move his head and front shoulders down to pick up the treat.

• As he is doing this, it is fairly easy then to push his hindquarters down so he achieves a total Down.

• Reward (praise, treat, clicker, etc.) then release him – "Off" or "OK".

With either training method, gradually extend the time that the puppy is held at the Down position. Wait until the puppy is totally secure in the Down with the handler standing close by, before attempting command at a distance. A second handler can be used to hold, then release the dog towards the first handler, who calls the dog's name, then "Down". Remember the reward.

The Down exercise and command can be combined with other commands. These include the formal "Wait" *(see page 202)* where the dog will rejoin the handler, or "Stay" where the handler will rejoin the dog. as well as the informal "Settle" *(see page 184)* where the dog is expected to stay down but not in a fixed position.

Note: The Down can be tested in competition from a stationary position or on the move, such as in Advanced Sit, Stand, Down, the Sendaway, in Agility and in Working Trials.

Down is essential Baic Contol. It can be a life-saver.

DUMB-BELL
A dumb-bell is a horizontal bar with two vertical ends, principally used in the Retrieve exercise.

The dumb-bell is designed to be easy for a dog to hold as the space provided by the two vertical uprights enables him to get his mouth around the bar without having to lift it from the ground.

Dumb-bells come in various sizes and materials. They are usually wooden, although there are some good plastic dumb-bells available. They may also be made of metal or have the central bar made of metal. The central bar itself is usually made of wood, but can be either of wood or metal, string whipped.

The vertical ends are usually square, but they may also be round or hexagonal.

CHOOSING A DUMB-BELL
• Use the square-ended variety as it is easier to control for distance (others may continue rolling).

The dumb-bell, the classic retrieve article, is easy for a dog to pick up and to hold.   *Photo: Brian McGovern.*

• Paint the ends white (not red, which is difficult for dogs to see) so that both dog and handler can see it in long grass.
• Ensure it is the right size for your dog, i.e. slightly wider between the uprights than your dog's mouth so that he can pick it up easily.

See Retrieve *(page 175)* for the pick-up and use of a dumb-bell.

ELECTRIC
See Collars – electric (page 111); Containment (page 114)

ELEMENTS
Modern training breaks each exercise into component elements and trains each individually. Only when each element is mastered are they trained together. Some exercises are then incorporated into others, e.g., Recall, into Retrieve, Retrieve into Scent.

EQUIPMENT
All Dogs.

AT HOME
Bed, Bedding: Avoid wicker baskets until your puppy has finished teething as they are eminently chewable! Most dogs prefer to sleep in a corner so that they have walls around them.
Crate, Indoor Kennel: Your pup's den. Highly desirable and safe for him and for the preservation of your possessions. Also excellent as an aid to house-training *(see House training page 149)*.
Bowls: For food and water. To avoid destruction, use metal bowls. You can buy bowls with attachments so that they can be fixed to the crate off the floor. These are particularly useful for the larger breeds as they avoid the animal putting undue strain on its shoulders.
Rewards: An indestructible bone for chewing, and toys for games (e.g. a ball on a rope, tennis ball, Kong, squeaky toy). Try to provide each of chase, chew and tug toys, plus small food treats, and clicker *(see Clicker training page 108)*.

Grooming equipment: To suit your particular breed/coat type.

IN THE CAR
Purpose-built cage or crate.
Barriers behind seat and before tailgate: Allows the back to be left up for air and contact.
Bowl for water: Remember that cars get very hot. Water must be available at all times.
Window guards: These enable the windows to be left wide open whilst ensuring that your pup does not escape through them.
See Containment page 114.

OUTSIDE
Collar: (leather, nylon, webbing, metal) with buckle and spring clip. May be either fixed, choke or half-choke *(see Collars page 111)*
Identity tag: Name address and phone number. Remember to change number when on holiday or following a move.
Lead: (leather, nylon, webbing) either short, long or Flexi.
Poop scoop: An essential to clean up after your dog.
Toy/rewards: At least one toy, so that you can have a game with your dog, some treats, and the clicker to use for rewards.

CONTROL
Halti or Figure of 8: If needed for control.
Muzzle (plastic or webbing): If your dog is aggressive.
Harness: Body harness.
Whistle: If your dog has been trained to respond to this signal.
Detergent bottle, water pistol, tin or discs: See Aversion *(page 87)*

SPORTS
All sports require specialist equipment.

OBEDIENCE
Collar: (either fixed or half-check is recommended).
Lead: Preferably webbing so that it can also be used as a toy and then washed.
Dumb-bell: Wooden or plastic with square ends so that it does not roll. *(see Dumb-bell page 130)*
Sendaway markers (usually four, but may be triangle or end).

Scent cloths (remember clean blanks).
Retrieve articles: For higher classes.

WORKING TRIALS
Tracking harness (leather or webbing) and 30 ft. line.
Dumb-bell: As in Obedience.
Tracking poles (6-8): To mark the Search Square for training Sendaway and to mark the start of the Track.
Articles for the Search Square and the Track: Lengths of hosepipe or tennis balls are ideal to start with.
Jumps: Scale (6 ft), Hurdle (3 ft) and Long Jump (9 ft).
Cap Pistol (for starting noise tolerence training, (*see page 162*).

FLYBALL
Hurdles (check which variety your club or team use).
Flyball machine.

AGILITY
Full set of Agility equipment (*see Agility page 76*).

FIELD TRIALS
Whistle.
Dummy (normally canvas-covered – may also be the floating type).
Access to gun and game.

SHEEPDOG TRIALS
Sheep.
A shepherd's whistle: To command the dog.
Hurdles: For driving the sheep through.
A pen: To pen the sheep.

FEEDING
See Rewards page 178; Bribery page 100.

FENCING
See Containment page 114.

FETCH
See Retrieve page 175.

FIELD TRIALS
A sport open to gundogs designed to assess their ability to work on live unhandled game, and where game may be shot.

The trials involve complex retrieving operations both on land and from water. There are various groups in a Field Trial.

RETRIEVERS AND WATER SPANIELS
Dogs are required to be steady by the handler whilst being shot over until commanded to search for dead or wounded game from land or water and retrieve gently to hand. Faults are:

Major	Elimination
Failing to find dead or wounded game	Hard mouth
Unsteadiness to heel	Whining or barking
Eye wipe	Running in or chasing
Disturbing ground	Out of control
Slack work	Failing to enter water
Noisy handling	Changing game whilst retrieving
whilst retrieving	Poor control

SPORTING SPANIELS
(Other than Irish Water Spaniels)
Dogs are required to quarter ground in quest of game, to be steady to flush shot and fall, and to retrieve gently on command from land or water. Faults are:

Major	Elimination
Failing to find game	Hard mouth
Not quartering and not	
making ground good	Whining or barking
Eye wipe	Missing game on the beat
Not stopping to shot and game	Running in and chasing
Disturbing ground	Out of control
Noisy handling	Failing to enter water
Poor control	Changing game whilst retrieving
	Catching unwounded game

POINTERS AND SETTERS
Dogs are required to quarter ground with pace and style in search of gamebirds, to point gamebirds, to be steady to flush and shot, and, where applicable, to fall. Faults include:

F

In Field Trials dogs, are marked on their method of working when retrieving game.

Photo: Graham Cox.

Major	Elimination
Not quartering and not making ground good	Flushing up wind
Not dropping to shot	Whining or barking
Stickiness on point	Missing gamebirds on the beat
Persistent false pointing	Chasing fur or feather
Not dropping to flush down wind	Out of control
Noisy handling	Unsteadiness to game
	Blinking a point

HUNT POINT AND RETRIEVE BREEDS
Dogs are required to quarter ground in search of game, to point game, to flush on command, to be steady to flush shot and fall, and to retrieve gently on command from land or water. Faults are:

Major	Elimination
Not making ground good	Hard mouth
Missing game on the beat	Whining or barking
Unsteadiness	Flushing up wind
Sticking on point	Running in and chasing
Not acknowledging game going away	Out of control
Failing to find dead or wounded game	Failure to hunt or point
Catching unwounded game	Missing gamebird on the beat
Disturbing ground	Refusal to retrieve or swim
Noisy handling	
Changing game whilst retrieving	

If you are interested in Field Trials, it is recommended that you join a club to view and understand the sport, and then get the specialist training needed.

FIGHTING
Some breeds of dog have a much higher propensity for

fighting than others, but in all breeds there will inevitably be some dogs who have this tendency.

EDUCATION
As with all other bad behaviour, this is best controlled in the early stages. Use basic training and socialisation. Encourage your puppy to play with other dogs when he is young so that he learns how to behave appropriately with his peers. Always remember that it is natural for dogs to play quite roughly and noisily with each other. Do not stop your pup from growling at his playmates, as this will only make him confused. Only active aggression needs to be stopped. Be severe if your puppy shows any sign of aggression. Command "No" or "Leave" as appropriate. Your reward must be instantaneous.

A SOLUTION
If you are unlucky enough to have a serious fighting problem within your own pack, there is a solution that has worked in a number of cases.

Separate the protagonists. Place them in runs on either side of a wire fence so that they cannot escape each other, nor can they actually connect with each other. You should then leave them in this situation for at least two hours. Do not interfere in any way, but leave the two to reach a conclusion.

I have tried this method successfully with two bitches that had a number of fights of increasing severity. At first they postured, growling and snarling at each other, running up and down the wire fence. However, at the end of the two-hour period, the stronger dog had out-faced the weaker, and the weaker dog was lying with her head down and turned away. They never fought again and lived together in complete harmony until one died of natural causes some years later.

As a point of interest, two male dogs will usually only fight for supremacy whereas two bitches will often fight to kill!

FIND
See Search page 181; Scent page 181.

FINISH
See Recall page 171.

FLYBALL
Flyball is an increasingly popular sport. It started originally in North America during the 1970s, and it is

now a major sport with over 7000 registered dogs. It is making rapid progress in Britain and elsewhere in Europe.

THE RULES
Two teams of dogs race over and jump hurdles in two adjacent, parallel lines. Each dog is sent by his handler across the start/finish line, over the four hurdles, to the Flyball box which contains a tennis ball. The dog presses the lever, and the box releases the ball. The dog catches the ball, retraces his steps over the hurdles with the ball in his mouth, and returns to the handler. Only then can the next dog in the team go.

Teams are usually made up of four dogs and handlers. The winners are the fastest without faults. Any type of dog, including crossbreeds, can do Flyball. Fitness is the only criterion. A Flyball dog is a happy dog.

There are already leagues and national competitions in the US, UK and elsewhere. Flyball will be one of the first UK sports to enter international competition when the British quarantine laws are lifted. There is already a commonality of rules (International Racing Rules Flyball) existing between Europe (Britain, Holland Germany and Belgium) with North America (USA and Canada), Japan, Australia and New Zealand.

TRAINING TECHNIQUES
Basic Control training is essential *(see page 91).*
• Initial training is with a primary motivator – a tennis ball. Ensure safety by making sure that the ball used is too large for your dog to swallow, and not too uncomfortable to hold. As with other dog sports, make your dog fanatical about his toys. Finding the ball and retrieving it must be an exciting and rewarding game for both dog and handler.
• Play rolling the ball and retrieving, gradually building up the distance. Ensure speed both in the outrun and in the recall. If your dog appears to be coming back more slowly in the recall than in the outrun, wind him up by running away at speed in

Flyball is a team sport, and the action is fast and furious.

Photo: Carol Ann Johnson.

137

the other direction so he will follow.
• An alternative is to throw a second article over your shoulder to keep your dog at full stretch. This second article (secondary motivator) can be a tug or similar article. When the dog retrieves it, have a vigorous game.
• Train the retrieve in its elements *(see page 175)*; the first element, the outrun is different from the Recall.
• Train the Recall without a Present (train the Present and "Give" separately).

A would-be player must then join a club or a team in order to use the correct equipment and to take part in team training.

GAMES
Games are vital for dogs. While humans play games to amuse themselves, all dogs play games to learn.

CATEGORIES
Games have been categorised by behaviourists into a number of groups. They include:
Chase games: e.g. you throw a ball, a toy, etc.; the dog chases retrieves and presents. Alternatively, your dog chases and then invites you to 'try' to get it back. When you chase your dog, he is then beginning to win the game.
Strength games: Tug of war, rugby etc. This may be played with a tug toy, or a ball on a rope, etc. When you let go, your dog wins.
Killing games: Your dog shakes the toy, stick, sock, scent cloth, etc. often with a growl.
Possession games: This is where your dog has 'won' one of the other games and then takes away the toy as a trophy. He may hide it, bury the bone, etc. or guard it in his 'den'.

PURPOSES
Each of these types of game is designed to teach the dog hunting and killing skills. All dogs play them and they are instinctive. If, as handlers, we understand the significance of these games, we can better control them in the behaviour shaping of our dogs.

If your dog is dominant, it is more important for you to win almost all of the games. If he appears wimpish and/or over-

Games are a vital part of the learning process.

Photo: Brian McGovern

submissive, it will help his self-esteem if he wins more often, which will, in turn, make him less submissive.

USING GAMES

Games are very important when teaching a new exercise. They can be incorporated either into the exercise itself or as part of the reward. You must teach your dog positively to play. Allocate one toy as a 'special toy'. A ball on a rope is useful as it can be used to throw or to tug.

It is important that games are initiated by you, and not by your dog. It is equally important that the toy belongs to you when you want a game rather than your dog. It must be regained and retained by you at the end of the game. As pack leader, you must control the whole game. The lead can also be used for a game – it is a plaything you always have available.

Remember the principle of intermittent reward when training existing or new exercises. Do not always have a game when an exercise has been correctly executed. Randomise the rewards.

"Control the game and you control the dog", John Rogerson.

GATE

Gates form a useful and sometimes necessary part of your dog's life.

Gate training reinforces the hierarchical position of the handler as pack leader by denying some access to the dog. This is particularly useful for conditioning dogs with a tendency to be over-dominant. It can also be used to help cope with separation anxiety *(see page 83)*. It is also a safety aid as a properly taught dog will not charge ahead into a field of livestock or some other potential hazard.

Outdoors/Field Gates
• With your dog on the lead, let him go through the gate, but close the door behind him with you still on the inside, holding the lead.
• Command your dog to "Sit", then "Wait" while you open the gate and go through. Call him through to "Close". Reward.
Obstacles: Gates are used as obstacles both for training sports either as hurdles to be cleared (Agility, KCJO, etc.) or as barriers to further progress. (Sheepdog Trials etc.). *See Agility page 76.*
Stairgate: The stairgate, commonly used to prevent children from going up or down stairs, is also of help to the dog trainer. It should be used at the bottom of stairs to limit access to certain parts of the house. It can also be used to render some areas 'dog free' for human allergy sufferers.

GOOD CITIZENS

UK
The Good Citizen Dog Scheme is the largest dog training scheme in the UK. Its aim is to promote responsible dog ownership and, in turn, to enhance the relationship between handler and dog. It also makes the community aware of the benefits associated with dog ownership.

The scheme brings together simple exercises as basic training (grooming, exercise, diet, cleaning up after the dog and general health care). All dogs are eligible for Good Citizen training, be they pedigree or cross breed, young or old. There are many organisations throughout the UK that co-ordinate the scheme including dog clubs, local councils, agricultural colleges, adult education centres, and British armed force bases.

The scheme incorporates three awards – Bronze, Silver and Gold. Each level involves a gradual development in understanding the behaviour and training of our dogs. They are described further below.

The Scheme is straightforward and non-competitive. On successful completion of each of the tests, participants are awarded a certificate to mark their achievement.

G

As the Kennel Club states "a trained dog is a happy dog", and remember, you *can* "teach an old dog new tricks".

Bronze Award	Silver Award	Gold Award
1. Cleanliness & identification	1. Play with Dog	1. Road walk
2. Collar and lead	2. Road walk	2. Return to handler's side
3. Walk on lead	3. Rejoin handler	3. Walk free beside handler
4. Control at door/gate	4. Stay in one place	4. Stay down in one place
5. Controlled walk through people and dogs	5. Vehicle control	5. Send the dog to bed
6. Stay down on lead	6. Come away from distractions (recall)	6. Stop the dog (instant down)
7. Grooming the dog	7. Controlled greeting (no jumping up)	7. Relaxed isolation
8. Present for examination	8. Food manners	8. Food manners
9. Return to handler	9. Examination of the dog	9. Responsibility and care.
10. Responsibility and care.	10. Responsibility and care.	

Further information may be obtained from dog clubs etc. and in particular the Kennel Club *(see Addresses page 208)* The Kennel Club recommends that every responsible dog owner participate in this Scheme.

USA

The AKC Canine Good Citizen Program ensures that "our favorite companion" is a respected member of the community. Over one million dogs have received their certificates since the inception of the program which covers both purebred and mixed breed dogs. It trains them to act with good manners in the home, in public places and in the presence of other dogs. Precision is not required: the program is non-competitive and is both fun and useful.

There are 10 steps

1. Accepting a Friendly Stranger. (Stranger speaks to and shakes hand with handler.)

2. Sitting politely for Petting. (Petting by a friendly stranger.)

3. Appearance and Grooming. (Both by owner and stranger e.g. a vet.)

4. Out for a Walk. (With the dog on a loose leash the handler must be in control for walking turns and a stop.)

5. Walking through a Crowd. (Both walk around and close to at least 3 people.)

6. Sit, Down on Command Staying in place. (While handler goes to end of 20 ft. line.)

7. Praise/Interaction. (Handler to calm dog after play and praise.)

8. Reaction to Another Dog. (Two handlers and their dogs to pass by each other.)

9. Reactions to Distractions. (Dog to be confident when faced e.g. by loud noise, jogger etc.)

10. Supervised Isolation. (Dog left attached to a 6 ft. line with a stranger for three minutes.)

Further information may be obtained from local clubs, the Scouts etc. and the American Kennel Club *(see Addresses page 208)* The AKC urges all dog owners to participate in this program.

GRASS-EATING
Although they are basically carnivores, dogs are, in fact, omnivores and will occasionally eat grass.

There appear to be two main reasons for grass-eating. One is to obtain nutrients, probably folic acid. The other is an emetic, to self-cure stomach trouble by vomiting both the grass and the other stomach contents. It is important to be aware of grass, wheat, etc. that has been sprayed with pesticides, and make sure your dog avoids it.

BREAKING THE HABIT
If your dog develops a habit of eating grass at other times, for example, during a Down Stay or in the Sendaway box in an Obedience competition, or when he is in the middle of another exercise away from the handler, then this must be stopped. Use standard techniques:-
• Aversion: Sound including the command "No" from another handler, or the use of tin-cans, discs etc.; Touch – squirting with a water-pistol, etc. *(see Aversion page 87)*.
• Sight-disapproving body language, scowl, etc. *(see page 97)*
• Distraction: Getting the dog to hold a toy or some other article in his mouth, which should then effectively prevent him from snacking on grass.

GROOMING ACCEPTANCE
Grooming is vital for dogs to stimulate the skin, give warning of impending problems, and indeed, to make dogs feel better. Grooming by the pack leader establishes the rank of each in the hierarchy.

Grooming must include the difficult but socially significant areas like the ears, feet, tail, top of neck, underparts etc. – 'no-go' areas cannot be permitted. Train the Stand *(page 190)* and use positive shaping and reinforcement with reward *(page 178)* when your dog stands still for grooming.

Provided grooming is properly taught, the dog will regard it as a good thing. He will appreciate the attention, he will be made more comfortable, and he will get a Reward at the end.

TIPS
• Start grooming as soon as your puppy arrives home, even if it is for just a few minutes at a time.
• Use a table or raised surface. If a dog is used to being on a table it will help when you visit the vet, and it can come in handy if you take part in Agility or breed competition. More importantly, it saves the handler's back!

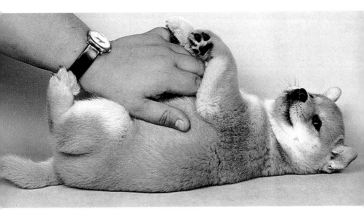

The puppy must accept handling – 'no-go areas' cannot be permitted.   *Photo: John Daniels.*

GUIDE DOGS FOR THE BLIND/SEEING EYE DOGS
The Guide Dogs for the Blind Association in the UK and the Seeing Eye in the United States are not only the oldest but probably the best known organisations to train dogs to aid the disabled.

The 'Seeing Dogs' are widely used by the visually impaired and they have become a familiar sight to many of us. Their importance to their handicapped handlers, and their level of training, has been recognised by legislation. Guide Dogs are allowed to accompany their handlers in places where dogs and other animals are otherwise forbidden – shops, restaurants, and other public meeting places.

TRAINING METHODS
The initial choice and training of guide dogs is similar to that

The guide dog must work calmly and sensibly amidst all the distractions of busy urban life.

Photo courtesy: Guide Dogs for the Blind Association.

of other service dogs. Dogs may be purchased or donated, or they may be bred specially. The breeds most commonly used are Labrador Retrievers, Golden Retrievers, Labrador/Golden crosses, and German Shepherd Dogs.

Puppies are usually placed in homes for the first year of their lives, where they can live a normal family life. During this time they are socialised with other dogs and people, and they are introduced to the situations that they will meet in later life, walking through crowds, getting used to traffic etc. At this time, they will also receive the Basic Control Training that all dogs require.

At the end of this stage, the dogs are taken into kennels where they receive the training that is appropriate for their future role. The duration of this may vary, but when they have reached a certain level of aptitude they will each be matched with their future blind owner, and the two will work together before finally qualifying.

GUNFIRE
All puppies should be assessed for their reaction to, and tolerance of, loud noises at an early age.

Obviously the greater the reaction and signs of nervousness, the more urgent the need for appropriate training. In fact, almost all dogs can overcome nervousness to loud noises (and therefore to gunfire) with suitable behaviour shaping.

Remember that dogs' hearing is far more acute than ours, and that they can hear higher frequencies (hence 'silent' dog whistles).

It is recommended that all dogs, particularly those that are likely to encounter gunfire or similar noises – fireworks, mining, quarrying, and even heavy traffic – should be trained to tolerate noise from puppyhood. (*See Noise tolerance page 162*)

Dogs should learn to tolerate noise from puppyhood.

Photo: Graham Cox.

These methods have had success with puppies descended from a long line of gun-shy dogs. If any dog still has problems with noise after receiving this training, it would be wise to consult a vet or a behaviourist.

HARNESS
A harness is an arrangement of straps around the body of a dog for attaching a line or other equipment.

A harness may be used on a dog for various purposes. These include handles on Guide Dogs (UK) or the Seeing Eye Dogs (US). It is used to attach a line for police trackers or for Working Trials. They may be used on particular breeds or where a dog has a problem with its neck.

Although usually used as an alternative to a collar and lead, a harness may be used in conjunction with them for specialist remedial training. There is a variety of halters and harnesses available to aid handlers who are unable to prevent their dogs from engaging in unwanted behaviour, particularly pulling. *(See Collars, page 111; Equipment page 131)*

HEARING DOGS FOR THE DEAF
This training scheme, where dogs act as 'ears' for their deaf owners, is becoming increasingly widespread, and is proving of immense benefit.

CHOICE AND TRAINING
It has been found that the best dogs for this work are those without strong guarding or hunting instincts, and in fact, cross-breeds have proved the most successful to date.

When chosen, puppies spend up to ten months with a

Socialiser, who teaches the dog Basic Control training and socialises it with children, other dogs, cats, and other animals. The dog is introduced to everyday aspects of life such as traffic, shops, etc. The dog then goes on to specialist training. During the course of this the dog is matched to a deaf owner and the two are trained together.

A hearing dog is trained to respond to a number of household noises; he alerts his owner by touching with a paw, and then leads the owner to the source. The hearing dog will respond to
• Doorbell.
• Telephone (specially adapted for the deaf).
• Cooker timer.
• Baby alarm.
• Smoke alarm.

Dogs of all sizes and all breeds have been successfully trained as Hearing Dogs for the Deaf.

Photo courtesy: Hearing Dogs for the Deaf.

HEELWORK
Walking to heel, both on and off the lead is essential Basic Control training. It is also recommend that you train it more formally, since it reinforces your position in the pack and inhibits pulling.

TRAINING TECHNIQUES
Heelwork can be trained in a small space and for short periods. Train:-
The Basic Position: Stand with your dog sitting stationary on your left.
Turns: Start in the stationary position and turn on the spot

through the turn, encouraging your dog into the stand and then back to the sit.

On the move: Only when you and your dog are proficient with the elements of turns on the spot should you attempt to do them on the move, and then only a pace away. Ensure there is no confusion in the mind of either you or your dog. If in doubt, go back to the Basic Position and static turns. Do not try fast pace until turns are thoroughly mastered at slow and normal pace

COMPETITIVE HEELWORK

To train more formal heelwork, use exercises to tighten the Basic Position, on the move. There are many books, videos, etc. on this one exercise, but briefly:-

• Use right hand circles to bring a lagging dog up to the Basic Position. Start with large circles and then decrease in size.
• Use left hand circles to bring a forward-working dog back to the Basic Position.
• Use horse dressage exercises to keep the dog thinking and using his feet correctly, e.g.

Serpentine: Walk a left hand semi-circle, then right hand semi-circle, with your dog changing his leading leg.

Side step: Move at right-angles, crossing left foot over right, with your dog following.

Backward: Handler and dog move backward (with a wall to the side to keep straight).

Figures of eight: Ensure the dog is in the Basic Position throughout.

Competition Heelwork requires precision and accuracy.

Photo: Brian McGovern.

Train at slow and normal paces then fast only when secure. Do not build in error.

HEELWORK TO MUSIC
See Canine Freestyle page 100.

HIERARCHY
See Pack Leader page 165.

HOLD
The command used when sending a dog out for a retrieve to ensure that the dog picks up the article cleanly and holds it in his mouth, without mouthing, when returning to the handler.
(See Retrieve page 175)

HOUNDS
Hounds are often used for hunting and racing. Some also make good pets.

PACKS
Foxhounds, Beagles, Otterhounds, Deerhounds, Basset Hounds .
Hunting with packs is documented as far back as the Middle Ages. Hounds are natural hunters and the huntsman simply harnesses their natural ability and controls it to the extent that each pack hunts a specific animal e.g. fox, hare, deer etc.

Voice control – the huntsman's horn, and the whippers-in – cracking their whips – control the hound pack.

Young hounds are often coupled to older hounds when they are first entered into the hunt. Most hounds do not make ideal pets, not because of any problem with their temperament, but simply because their instinct to hunt is so strong that hounds are prone to stray after a scent and it is extremely difficult for any handler to overcome this.

All of these types of hound have phenomenal scenting ability and hunt entirely by nose.

INDIVIDUAL
Greyhound, Whippet, Afghan Hound, Saluki
These breeds hunt by sight. They are all extremely fast and will run down their prey – usually a hare. There has been a decline in hunting natural prey and a huge increase in artificial lure racing. Greyhound and Whippet racing are extremely

The Greyhound hunts by sight, and this can be channelled into chasing an artificial lure.   Photo: Steve Nash.

popular sports and provide an excellent family evening out. These breeds generally make excellent loving pets. They have delightful temperaments but may be uncertain with cats.

The training of hounds for their particular sport is a specialist activity beyond the scope of this book. Their training as pets is covered by the various Basic Control exercises *(see page 91)*, and standard techniques *Diversion, page 122; Aversion, page 87 and Containment page 114)*

HOUSE TRAINING
Among the first lessons a puppy must learn is that of cleanliness.

Most animals born in a nest or den have an instinct to move away from the den to relieve themselves. Indeed, they will do so as soon as they are able. Dogs will begin to leave the sleeping area after about three to four weeks.

We can take advantage of this 'pre-programming' by shaping a puppy's behaviour to consider the entire house as his den, and that therefore he must go outside the house to relieve himself.

TRAINING TECHNIQUES
Training should start as soon as you get the puppy home. Take him outside to the same spot in your garden/yard:
• First thing in the morning, last thing at night, and at least once every hour.

Allocate an area in your garden which can be used for toilet training.

Photo: Sheila Atter.

- Shortly after each feed.
- Immediately after play and exercise.
- Immediately after any excitement – new faces, dogs, visitors, etc.
- Immediately after waking.

The puppy should be allowed to wander and sniff around. This expedites the process. You must be patient and accompany your puppy. If you put him out on his own, his immediate reaction is to get back to join you, i.e. inside the house.

A puppy is easily distracted and may forget why he wanted to go out in the first place. Unfortunately he is likely to remember as soon as he is inside. This results in a mess in the house and an untrained dog.

So put on your coat, get your umbrella if needs be, and go out with your puppy. Reward him for success outside with praise, a treat, etc. Start to shape his behaviour for the future by adding to the praise your key word – for example, "Be Clean" – which you intend to use in public when the dog has been trained to relieve himself on command.

Although you need to stay outside with your puppy, there is no need to stay there for hours. If he shows no signs of performing, bring him back in positively. Take him out again as soon as he shows tell-tale signs, such as sniffing, circling, squatting, etc.

CRATE/INDOOR KENNEL

Use the crate as an indoor kennel during the early months. If you put the puppy's bed inside the crate, he soon learns that it is his den, and not to be soiled. Use the other half of the crate to lay newspapers. Your puppy will soon learn to leave his bed and urinate/defecate only on the newspaper. When he is older, dispense with the playpen/newspaper area, leaving the crate solely as his den. This will aid the training process, so that the puppy learns to wait to go outside to relieve himself.

ACCIDENTS WILL HAPPEN

 If you catch your puppy in the act, give a shout. This will distract him from his performance. After the shout, rush away, calling his name, excitedly, enthusiastically to the back door. Go outside to his 'spot', wait until he has relaxed from the excitement whereupon he will finish what he started earlier. Reward in the usual way. Then go inside. Put the pup in a separate room while you clean up the mess.

It is important to eliminate the scent after an accident. Dogs are programmed with their remarkable sense of smell to use the spot again. As we trained the puppy to use his spot outside in the early stages, so we must discourage him from using a spot inside. This will mean not only cleaning up the mess, but also using an odour eliminator. This can be obtained from most pet suppliers. A biological washing powder solution, preferably hot, will also help.

PUNISHMENT

Accidents will happen but will happen considerably less if the puppy's behaviour is shaped positively using the rewards, rather than negatively by using punishment. It is simply an old wives' tale that rubbing the puppy's nose in his mess that was done earlier will stop it in future. A puppy will not learn from this or any other punishment meted out after the event because a dog cannot, of course, relate the punishment he is receiving with an earlier act.

It is another old wives' tale to believe the puppy looks guilty and therefore he knows he has done wrong. The pup is, in fact, looking submissive to appease his pack leader whose body language radiates anger. This submissive display may look like anthropomorphic guilt.

Not only is delayed punishment ineffective it may, in fact, be counter-productive. If your dog is constantly afraid that you will show anger to him for an unexplained reason, he will become insecure and unhappy. This, in turn, may make for more submissive behaviour including submissive urination. The cycle will only get worse!

HOW LONG?
Different dogs learn at different rates. Some may be house trained literally within days of coming home. Others may take up to six months or more. Perhaps the biggest influence on this timing is the amount of time and effort put into his behaviour shaping by you, his trainer. More input speeds up the time taken and less will, of course, delay it.

OUTSIDE THE HOME
Dog faeces is one of the most common causes of complaint amongst non-dog lovers. They have a valid point. Faeces can carry toxocara canis which can infect children.

Nobody likes treading in, or otherwise being in contact with dog faeces. Every one of the 20 million dogs in the USA and over 6 million dogs in the small crowded island of Britain has to defecate every day. In the USA, the UK, and many other countries, national or local ordinances make it an offence to leave dog mess in public places. We must be responsible dog owners and ensure that our dog's faeces are correctly dealt with. Make sure you always carry the means to do this (plastic bags, pooper-scoop etc.)

TIPS
• Toilet training on command: Train your dog to excrete on command. Use the house training chosen phrase, like "Be Clean". Remember the Reward.
• Appropriate areas: Reward your dog for performing in long, rough grass or undergrowth, if that is acceptable in your environment.
  Be Responsible. Bag it and bin it.

HUNTING
See Hounds page 148.

HURDLE
Obstacle used in various sports including Working Trials (3 ft high), Agility (2 ft high), Obedience in US and in KCJO plus retrieves (2 ft), Flyball plus retrieve (withers less 4 ins), Sheepfog Trials (as a fence equivalent).

I

IDENTIFICATION
A dog must wear a collar with a name-tag in many jurisdictions of the USA and all of the UK.

You must comply not only to stay within the law but also for the safety of your pet. Traumas can happen – a burglar or a car thief may release your dog away from your home. A car crash may leave your dog running in a blind panic on the freeway, sudden noise e.g. fireworks on July 4th or Guy Fawkes night may cause a bolt. A means of identification will reunite you. In addition to the name plate or tag with your name, address and phone number on the collar, consider:
• Tattooing – it is indelible.
• Microchipping – gives a unique ID.
• DNA profiling – increasing in popularity, particularly with breeders.

INDOOR KENNEL, PEN
If your puppy is to live indoors, it is a good idea to borrow or buy a large folding cage/crate to use as an indoor kennel/crate.
See Containment page 114; Crate-training page 117.

INTERNATIONAL COMPETITION
Sport and competitions for man and his dog have developed on insular national lines. This has arisen largely as a result of anti-rabies quarantine laws in the UK and elsewhere, and by national regulatory bodies. It is now likely that the quarantine laws will be replaced with vaccination, a pet passport and probably microchipping, so the route to international competition will open up.

It is not too fanciful to have Grand Prix, European, Commonwealth, Pan-American, Ryder Cup, World Cup, even Olympic events. As there are horse trials at international level, so there will be canine equivalents.

There are sports which already have a commonality of rules. Examples are:

Flyball: Already has a commonality of rules between the USA, the UK, and continental Europe.

Agility: This is, or can be, commoned up between the UK, Europe and North America.

Obedience: This will provide more of a problem since it has developed separately in the UK and the US. In the UK it is more like the equine dressage competition with the emphasis on precision, while in the US it has more exercises.

Working Trials: This sport is already being developed on each side of the Atlantic, but, here again, work will have to be done to produce a common sport.

Canine Freestyle (USA)/Heelwork to Music (UK): This is the newest canine sport, but international competition is likely, perhaps initially by video-linking.

J

JUMPING UP

Jumping up, particularly at people but also at other dogs, is a behaviour which is not to be tolerated and which must be reshaped.

Puppies jump up to solicit food from their pack leaders, and in exuberant submissive greeting to other members of their pack. This behaviour looks and, indeed, is appealing to humans since the pup's obvious pleasure at seeing us makes us feel good too. However, not everybody appreciates this gesture, particularly if done with dirty paws.

There is also a more serious implication. Jumping up by a pup will become a dominance trait in an older dog. It establishes his rank and inhibits movement of you as an inferior. While it is important not to flatten natural exuberance, the dog's behaviour must be shaped against jumping.

TRAINING TECHNIQUES

The standard techniques can be used to prevent jumping up:

Diversion: Use positive training commands, e.g.

• "Sit" before the dog jumps up. A dog who is sitting cannot jump up. Reward as soon as the dog is sitting, then train him to "Wait" at the "Sit" or "Down".

• Train the instant "Down" so that you, or another handler, can drop the dog to the Down at a distance, before he jumps at some unsuspecting stranger. Reward when the dog is down and waiting in position for you.

• Get down to your dog's level rather than staying erect, which will only provoke the dog to jump. Crouch, sit on the floor, whatever.

• A reflex response to "Come" to you is also a diversion. See "Sit" and "Down" for this Basic Control training *(page 91)*.

Aversion:

• Touch – Use a squirt of water from your water pistol or detergent bottle aimed while the dog is jumping up, followed by a reward as reinforcement when he is on four feet.

The old-fashioned method of touch was to bring the handler's knee up to the dog's chest as he jumped. This required better timing than most handlers can produce, and, in isolated instances, was dangerous to the dog's breast-bone

Hearing – Train the sound aversion technique of behaviour reshaping with the use of the keys, tin can, or discs to have the dog recalled to the handler instead of leaping at visitors or strangers *(see page 87)*. Consider a whistle.

Containment: Basic Control training with collar and lead should prevent your dog jumping up at strangers, and if used in the house, at visitors. Use the crate, particularly during the initial excitement of the visitor's arrival and greeting before the puppy or dog is introduced to the melee.

JUMPS
These are names of groups of obstacles in specific sports e.g. Working Trials, Agility, KCJO. etc.
See Equipment page 131. and relevant sports.

KENNEL CLUB – UK
Canine activities are governed and regulated by the Kennel Club.

Its sphere of influence is extensive: The Kennel Club is responsible for the following:

• Breed registrations.

• Licensing shows.

• Framing and enforcement of rules which cover Obedience, Working Trials, Field Trials, Agility, Flyball as well as Breed Shows.

- Publishing Breeds Standards.
- Operating Junior Organisations (KCJO) and Good Citizen Dog Schemes.
- Funding research projects.
- Running a canine library
- Publishing the monthly *Kennel Gazette*
- Running Crufts as "the world's greatest dog show".

KENNEL CLUB JUNIOR ORGANISATIONS (KCJO/AKCJO)

These organisations encourage young people between the ages of 8 and 18 to take an interest in the training, behaviour and care of dogs, and to enjoy all activities connected with dogs. They promote courtesy, sportsmanship, loyalty and self-discipline. They help youngsters learn a sense of responsibility in canine activities.

Visits to shows, trials, dog training centres, local kennels, sanctuaries are organised, as well as other canine events and competitions being run during the year and at Crufts and Westminster. Importantly, a youngster does not have to own a dog to join – you just need to be interested in the world of dogs.

Further information can be obtained from KCJO Kennel Club (UK), and from American Kennel Club (US). *See Addresses page 208.*

KENNELLING
See Boarding page 96.

LAW
It is essential that anyone owning a dog is aware of both their legal responsibilities and their rights with regard to their pet.

UK
Noise: A large percentage of the complaints made to the authorities relate to noise nuisance caused by barking dogs.
Strays: Numerous road traffic accidents are caused by dogs straying on to the highway.

L

Attacks: There have been a number of high-profile attacks, or alleged attacks, by dogs on members of the public. As a result of these cases, laws have been introduced to govern responsibility for a dog's behaviour. *See Dangerous Dogs page 119.*

A 'keeper' (the dog's 'owner' or 'possessor') will be liable for damage caused by the dog which results in the death of or injury to a person and also to inanimate objects. He remains as keeper of the dog until someone else fulfilling these qualifications succeeds him. (A person who takes possession of a dog to prevent it causing damage or to restore it to its owner does not become its keeper just because of that possession.)

It is recommended that any person whose dog has caused damage should take legal advice before admitting any liability.

USA

Although the law relating to dogs varies from state to state, the American Kennel Club favours reasonable, enforceable and non-discriminatory laws governing the ownership of dogs.

Dog owners are actively encouraged to confine and properly control their dogs at all times. In addition, they are expected to clean up after their dog and, in many cases, to keep their dogs on a lead whenever they are in a public place.

Just as in UK, dog owners may well be liable for damage caused by their dog, and all owners must be aware of their responsibilities in this regard.

The AKC works tirelessly with other animal groups to support legislation that protects purebred dogs and to speak out effectively against laws that are not in the best interests of purebred dogs.

LEAD, LEASH, LEAD-TRAINING
A dog's lead is a line fixed to his collar at one end and held by his handler at the other. It is a legal requirement outdoors. It is an essential aid for training.

A lead or leash has a fastener (pistol, snap, etc. at its end) to connect to the ring on the collar. It comes in a variety of materials: leather; chain; webbing (cotton or nylon); rope; man-made fibre, etc. Its length will vary (sometimes long for some training, flexi- etc). *See Equipment page 131.*

A lead's importance in training cannot be over-emphasised. It is one of the aids for direct communication with your dog and the means of control.

TRAINING TECHNIQUES
Start lead training indoors as soon as possible after your puppy has settled in. As always, use rewards.
• Put on his collar and, when he is used to it, attach his lead just before his meal. Place the bowl on the floor and lead the pup to it. Leave the lead on while the pup eats.
• Put on the lead before a visitor enters the house. After the initial excitement and human greetings, allow the pup to greet the visitor while on the lead. The puppy soon learns that the lead means excitement and reward.
• When you and your dog are used to the lead indoors, train in your garden/yard. To begin with, you may find that your puppy makes a huge fuss of the lead, bucking and straining or throwing himself on his back, but you must persevere.
• Walk in a wide left-hand circle with your puppy on your left side and the lead held loosely. Do not be surprised if he tries to leap around you – quietly go on walking.
• Give lavish praise when, by accident, the puppy lands by your left leg (the position you eventually want him to take), and say the "Close" or "Heel" followed by a reward ("Good Boy") in an excited voice, use of the clicker, a treat etc.).
• Do not keep the lead short at this stage – let the puppy learn the extent of his freedom. Once he is confident of the lead and no longer fighting it, you can incorporate a small flick of the lead when he starts to pull so that he learns that this is not a good thing to do.

Work on lead-training in your garden, and then the puppy will be confident when you venture into the outside world.

Photo: Lyn Kipps.

- Once your puppy is walking confidently on the lead in the garden (and he has completed his inoculation course), you can venture into the outside world. Then (when he has had his inoculations), train in the outside world.
- Remember to make haste slowly, and stop pulling from the outset (*See Pulling page 168*)

LEADERSHIP
See Pack Leader page 165.

LICKING
Dogs lick each other, and humans. Dogs lick for various reasons, but licking visitors to the house, or even strangers, can be a cause of embarrassment.

   One of the main reasons for licking is a submissive gesture from the lower ranking wolf to the higher. Where there is a mutual licking session, this is usually initiated by the pack leader, or other high-ranking animal.

Puppies' submissive licking appeals to humans. We regard it anthropomorphically as kissing. In practice, of course, the puppy who starts by being submissive finds that licking produces reward through affection – patting, etc. This naturally continues in later life, when his behaviour may well become dominant. As few of us tell off our dogs for what looks like a show of love, we reinforce our dogs' behaviour, shaping him to lick us by giving him 'grooming' when he provokes us to give the desired response.

TRAINING
You can reshape your dog's behaviour against excessive licking by using the standard aversion or diversion techniques.

Diversion: See Diversion *(page 122)* but briefly: -
- Use the "Sit" or "Down" command and then reward him for the Sit.
- Watch the dog's body language. If you are able to stop the licking in time, you or the visitor can divert him with a toy or game. Use the "Hold" command – if a dog is holding an article, he cannot be licking.

Aversion: See Aversion *(page 87)* for detailed training, but briefly: -
• Taste – Use tabasco, bitter apple or equivalent. Soak a tissue in bitter apple and pop it into your dog's mouth. Let go. Your dog will spit it out and try to get rid of the unpleasant taste. Have a dilute solution of bitter apple in a clean scent or detergent bottle. Spray willing volunteers. Your dog will recoil.
• Touch – Arm the visitor with a water-pistol or a detergent bottle filled with water to squirt on the dog's nose.
• Hearing – Use sound aversion (the tin-can, rattle or discs) to change the dog's behaviour.

LONG JUMP
This is an obstacle in certain competitions e.g. Working Trials, Police Trials and Agility. The jump technique required is usually a long, low parabola (as opposed to the hurdle, for example).
See the relevant sport e.g. Agility (page 76) for details.

MEDIA DOGS
The wolf came out of the wild to become 'man's best friend', and he immediately became part of man-made culture. Portrayals have ranged from cave paintings through Roman and Greek mythology to modern times. Today dogs are widely used in advertisements, as well as taking starring roles in television and films.

The majority of 'media dogs' are highly trained. Their training consists of:
Basic Control Training: Including the standard Recall ("Come"), instant response to the Sit and Down, walking to heel ("Close"), and response to the leave commands ("Leave" and "No").
Advanced Training: Leaving the handler on command (Sendaway), adopting positions on command away from the handler (Advanced, Sit, Stand, Down), working on both hands of the handler i.e. both left and right (as in Agility).
Agility and Stunts: Depending on what is needed, dogs may also need to perform agility tasks. For example, jumping over

Cassacre Berwick Of Cripton: A top performing TV/film dog, owned and trained by Pat Barker.

furniture, obstacles etc. in chase scenes ("Over"), barking on command ("Speak"), being quiet on command or signal, ("Quiet"), and retrieving ("Fetch") a variety of objects.

To be successful media dogs must have:-

Flexibility: A media dog must be biddable and easily trained to new tasks called up by the script and the director. These may include the equivalent of manwork in Working Trials (jumping at a criminal etc.), working in water, swimming across lakes, and many other tasks.

Temperament: The dog, and indeed the handler, must have the right temperament. Directors of film and television are not noted for their consideration towards human actors, let alone making allowances for canine actors. Both dog and handler must be prepared for endless retakes, with tedious waits between activity.

In particular, the dogs must be thoroughly socialised with people, children and other animals. They must be trained to be noise-tolerant, not only for human voice and shouting but also for the bangs and crashes that happen on sets.

Owners/handlers who are interested in their dogs performing in the media (and they may themselves get walk-on parts) should contact one of the agencies who specialise in this work. Most companies who require animals in their productions go through such an agent to get the animals they require.

MOTIVATION
See Rewards page 178; Attitude page 86.

MUSIC
See Canine Freestyle/Heelwork to Music page 100.

NOISE TOLERANCE
You must train your puppy to be used to noise, both general and specific, and both indoor and outdoor. Many dogs are gun-shy or frightened of thunder. In the majority of cases, this shyness could have been eliminated if the dogs were correctly trained and noise-introduced from the beginning.

TRAINING TECHNIQUES
Remember that dogs are far more sensitive to sound than humans. They can hear sounds farther away and at a higher frequency. Start training/shaping: -
Indoors: Introduce your puppy to the vacuum cleaner and other domestic noises, washing machines, etc. If your puppy exhibits nervousness, then gentle training will help.
• With your pup close by you, make a deliberate noise by banging two objects together. Simultaneously reward the puppy "Good boy", and start a game.
• Progress to rattling the food bowl before a meal and banging a tin tray. As with all training, do not progress too fast.
Outdoors: The training is equally important. While the pup must learn to distinguish between the bewildering variety of noises of the outside world, he must also be taught not to be frightened of noise itself, or any specific noise. Shape him gently to outdoor noises by training:
• Have your pup close by you when you come across easily identified small noises. Progress slowly to louder noises.
• Use diversion (game, toy) and rewards. Progress to cars, traffic, aeroplanes, guns, etc.
• Use a tape containing thunder, gunfire, etc. playing softly at first while you feed your dog. Increase the volume very slowly over a period of time.
   These techniques do work – try them positively.

NOISE/NUISANCE
To keep a dog that causes substantial discomfort or annoyance may give rise to a civil action for nuisance. Most nuisance caused by dogs results from excessive barking.

The authorities often make regulations and bylaws to deal with a person who keeps a noisy animal in any house, building or premises which may cause a serious nuisance to residents in the neighbourhood.

Many organisations which control public open spaces also have regulations detailing how an owner should control his dog (e.g. kept on a lead, not disturb or worry any bird or animal).

See Barking page 90. Ideally, teach him "Speak" to bark and "Quiet" to stop.

You must keep your dog under control and prevent him from being a noise nuisance.

NOSEWORK
See Tracking page 197; Search page 181.

OBEDIENCE
Obedience is "the practice of obeying, willingness to obey orders" *(Collins).* **It is also the name of the competitive sport.**

OBEDIENT DOGS
We must strive to have obedient, good pack member dogs. Teach your dog Basic Control *(page 91).* Learn and apply the training techniques; Positive shaping – see Rewards (page 178), Diversion *(page 122)*, Aversion *(page 87),* and, if necessary, Containment *(page 114)*

OBEDIENCE – THE SPORT
This is the biggest canine teamwork sport in the UK and the USA, and it is growing in popularity elsewhere e.g. Holland, Germany and Australia. There are national differences:
• Entries - In the USA entry is restricted to purebred dogs, while in the UK it is open to all, including crossbreeds and pedigree unregistered dogs, but all Obedience dogs have to be on a working register.
• Exercises – There are exercise differences: e.g. in the US, the retrieve is over hurdles; this is not the case in the UK (except KCJO). The Scent tests differ, and in the UK the

Heelwork is extremely precise, akin to dressage for horses.
• Judging control standards vary, with more personal latitude taken for example in the UK than in Germany.

These differences in rules and their interpretation must be addressed before full-scale international competition can take place.

THE EXERCISES
Tested exercises in Obedience Shows/Trials are carried out with commands in the lower classes, but without commands in the higher classes, briefly:-

Heelwork: Dog and handler work close together, on and off the lead, with turns, about turns, and halts. In advanced classes, the exercise must be performed at slow, normal and fast paces, and ASSD (Advanced Sit, Stand, Down) and pick-ups.

Retrieve: The handler throws a dumb-bell (other articles in senior classes) with the dog at the Sit by your side in the Basic Position. Send your dog out to pick up article, retrieve it to your front and present. He must give the article to you and finish on command.

Recall: The dog is left in the Sit or Down and is then called/signalled back to the handler who is stationary in lower classes and on the move in the higher classes.

Sendaway: The dog is sent (from Basic Position) to a designated spot and commanded to an instant Down.

Distant Control: The dog is stationary while the handler moves away. The dog is commanded to adopt the Sit, Down, Stand positions in the order prescribed by the judge.

Temperament: The dog must be trained to submit to being approached and patted by the judge.

Obedience exercises become progressively more difficult as dog and handler graduate up the classes.

Stays: The dog must stay in one place in the designated position (Stand, Sit, or Down) for specific periods of time, while the handler must first turn his back (lower classes) and go out of sight (higher classes).

Scent: The dog must pick up and retrieve a cloth scented by the handler (lower classes) or the judge (higher classes). The dog must discriminate it from a number of other cloths, some of which are unscented and one or two others are 'decoy' (scented by others).

GETTING STARTED
Join an Obedience Club which has a competition section – addresses from your national Kennel Club *(see Addresses page 208)* In addition to you and your dog, you will need
• Collar and lead.
• Rewards (treats, toy, clicker, whistle, etc.).
• A dumb-bell (your club will advise), this will be required later on in training.
Basic Control: Before you think of Obedience competition, you must train the exercises listed under Basic Control *(see page 91)*

FURTHER TRAINING
In addition to training at your club, there are books, courses and videos purely on competitive Obedience.
Shows (UK), Trials (US): Prepare for your competitive career by entering your club's internal competitions, then progress further up the ladder as you gain in experience.

OBSTACLES
These may be natural as in walking shooting, etc. or they may be made for competition.
See Agility *(page 76)*; Field Trials *(page 134)*; Flyball *(page 136)*; KCJO *(page 156)*; Sheepdog Trials *(page 185)*; Working Trials *(page 204)*

PACK LEADER
Descended from the wolf, the dog is, and remains, a pack animal. Each pack must have a clearly recognised pack

**leader. In today's anti-dog world, the pack leader must
not be your dog – it must be you.**

RESPONSIBILITIES
As the human pack leader, you not only have authority over
your pack, including your dog, but you must also accept
responsibility for it. The famous saying "A dog is for life and
not just for Christmas" encapsulates your responsibilities for
the provision of food, grooming, shelter, protection, safety,
health care etc. for your dog. The best pack leaders are
benevolent dictators – tolerant and friendly, but
uncompromising when needs be.

In today's world dogs are often given privileges of rank
(food, bed, mating, winning games, etc.) which would be
denied them in the wild. This may give the dog the belief that
he is higher in his pack's hierarchy than, in fact, he is or
should be. A number of these hierarchical ranking activities,
and how they should be handled by you as pack leader, are
highlighted under Dominance *(page 125)*.

As pack leader, you must know your hierarchy. Be aware of
the predilection of some of your pack to assume dominance
or to vie for pack leadership. Equally you should be aware
that other members of your pack, dogs included, may be
overly submissive and have a view of their position in the
pack in the other direction i.e. they feel that they are more
inferior than in practice they need to be.

Your responsibilities are not only for providing for your
pack, but also for shaping behaviour i.e. training the dog to

As pack leader, you have clearly defined responsibilities.
Photo: Amanda Bulbeck.

accept his role within your pack and to conform to its rules. Re-shape both over-dominance and over-submissiveness and anxiety.

You must give your dog Basic Control training *(see page 91)*, and take part in your relevant Good Citizens Scheme/Program *(see page 140)* . *Keep shaping and training. You and your dog will enjoy and benefit from it.*

PEN
See Crate-training page 117; Containment page 114.

POLICE DOGS
The training of dogs used in police work, together with other service dog training, formed the springboard for modern training today.

The needs of the police force are wide-ranging, and dogs are used in many different roles, such as sniffing for drugs and explosives, search and rescue, patrol work, criminal work, as well as for general public relations exercises. The German Shepherd Dog is still the most popular breed for the majority of these tasks, although other breeds, such as Spaniels and Retrievers, are more often used for 'sniffer' work.

The police dog must receive Basic Control training with instantaneous response to his handler. The dog must be sound in mind and body, and show the right Attitude *(see page 86)*. He must be courageous, but his aggression must always be under tight control.

Police dogs must show a high degree of courage.

Obviously, the dogs who are used for the more specialised disciplines, such as drug/explosive detection, receive appropriate training.

POSSESSION
See Dominance (page 125); Games (page 138)

PRAISE
See Rewards (page 178)

PREVENTION
Prevention is the fourth major area of technique in dog training. It is commonsense that if you cannot otherwise reshape your dog, you must prevent him from taking an unwanted action.
See Containment (page114) for detailed methods of prevention.

PULLING
Pulling on the lead is one of the most common complaints of the dog handler.

The problem usually arises from dominance. Remember that the pack leader's responsibilities include protection and leadership. If your dog is dominant, he will lead and protect his perceived lower ranking pack members (i.e. you!), particularly when away from his den (home).

Pulling is a sign of dominance, and must be corrected.

P

RESHAPING

Reshape your lifestyle by a dominance reduction programme. Reinforce your position as pack leader by assuming the privileges of rank. See Dominance *(page 125)* for reshaping and training techniques, but briefly look at the following areas:

Doorways, hallways, gates: Ensure you go first, your dog goes second. He gets out of your way.

Furniture (including bed): Make sure you sit, etc. where you want. The dog does not sleep on your bed or your chair.

Food: Do not allow your dog to beg, feed him after you have eaten, or at a totally different time.

Games and toys: Make sure you initiate and stop games. Ensure 'His' toy is *yours*, and *you* retain it after a game.

Outdoors: Ensure that you control your garden/yard, and that there are no 'no go' areas.

OTHER TRAINING TECHNIQUES

Heelwork: Train your dog to walk in the Basic Position (his shoulder near your left leg) and to walk to heel both on the lead and heel free. When your dog pulls, you halt him to heel "Close". Then do some formal Heelwork, including turns, before continuing informally.

Reining: This technique comes, as do many canine techniques, from horse training. Use your lead as a rider uses his reins to slow a galloping horse. As your dominant dog pulls and you resist, he will pull harder (action/reaction). So as your dog pulls, release suddenly: he will then lurch forward and break his stride. Take up the slack of the lead and then repeat as necessary. Releasing a loop of lead held in your hand in readiness aids the technique.

The Flexi-lead can be worked on the same principle: take off the ratchet. Your dog will run free. Partly apply the brake which runs over the ratchet, causing the lead to wobble. This, in turn, makes the dog wobble and break his stride.

This technique shows your dog that he cannot win because there is nothing to pull against, and that when he tries to run or walk faster than you, he wobbles foolishly.

Leadership: Another technique is to change direction by 180 degrees. Your dog will then have to watch you to see in which direction you are leading.

Proprietary equipment: In view of the scale of the problem, proprietary leads, collars and harnesses have been designed for handlers who find the above techniques beyond them.

These include: Flexi-lead (used as above), Col-leash, Figure of 8, Halti (halter), Harness, etc.

Try reshaping techniques first, but if you still have problems, try one of these aids.

PUNISHMENT
Punishment seems to be humans' favourite training method. It is not effective.

MISUSE

Beat the child; jail the thief, bomb the dictator. The fact that these are not effective methods is proved by the continuance of ill-behaved children, criminals, dictators, etc. They are even less effective with dogs than with humans since humans can reason logically and relate present punishment to past crime. Dogs cannot. Two examples:

Example I: You return home and find that your dog has had a fine time chewing your slippers, and is now asleep in his bed. If you punish him now you may reinforce his chewing since, in his eyes, he is being punished for sleeping – not for chewing which is still OK.

Example II: Your dog chases a child across the park. The child's mother is, understandably, frightened and annoyed. You recall the dog and punish him for his behaviour. Here again, your dog perceives that he is being punished for coming to you – not for chasing which is still OK.

Dogs learn through the positive reinforcement of reward. So use these methods rather than the old 'shout and beat' routine.

Do not fall into the trap that humans often do of:
• Using punishment to reinforce your dominance over your dog.
• As a revenge against your dog.
• Before your dog has understood what is required in his training.

USES

Punishment does have its training uses, but it must only be used very early in behaviour, sparingly and suddenly. For example, you must teach your dog not to bite you – or any humans. However gently he holds your arm, shout suddenly, loudly. If he persists, do as his mother in the pack would do: pick him up by the scruff of his neck, shake him and let go.

Only use this technique if you are more than 110 per cent certain that your dog is disobeying you wilfully, and from a lack of respect. Then consider your respective positions carefully and embark on a dominance reshaping programme. *See Dominance page 125.*

QUIET
"Quiet" is an essential command for many dogs, particularly those prone to barking.
See Barking (page 90) and Speak (page 189).

RANK
See Dominance page 125; Pack Leader page 165.

RECALL
The Recall is Basic Control training that is essential for all dogs. Nothing is more annoying than a dog that will not come when he is called.

ELEMENTARY TRAINING
Start shaping as soon as you bring your puppy home: -
Mealtimes: When you are about to feed, kneel down and call your puppy's name and give the command "Come". Rattle the feed bowl at the same time, and he will almost certainly come to you at once. Reward him excitedly "Good boy", and give him his food. Do this at every mealtime.
Play: You will quickly find that when you play with your puppy, he comes running towards you. Do not waste this opportunity – call his name with the command "Come", and give the appropriate reward as soon as he responds.
Be Positive: At this stage, do not call your puppy to you for anything he might object to, like bedtime or restricting his freedom, as you will only encourage him to disobey. *Never* punish the puppy when he comes to you after misdemeanours committed elsewhere, or you will very soon find that he will not respond.

Elementary Recall training can start as soon as your puppy arrives home.

Shaping: Call your puppy by name, command "Come", and reward. This will shape and reinforce his behaviour to learn that coming to you is pleasurable and preferable to doing his own thing. Later, when he has fully learnt this, give rewards randomly and unpredictably to keep him keen.

LATER LIFE – THE WAIT ELEMENT
Give your puppy a chance to mature before progressing. Then train the Wait.
• With the dog in the Basic Position *(see page 91)*, place him in the Sit giving the command "Sit" firmly. Ensure that he is sitting tidily with his feet neatly under him, and his tail straight out behind him. Do not let him lean on to your leg. As in Heelwork, his front feet should be level with your instep, and his bottom exactly straight with your legs.
• Command "Wait" holding the lead in your left hand, above the dog's head. Take a half-pace away from him to the right, ensuring by use of the lead and your left hand that he does not move. Silently count to five, and then turn to the dog and praise him, while still ensuring that he does not move from the Sit position.
• Gradually increase the distance you move away from him to the side, the front and the back of him, keeping him on the lead at all times and making quite sure that he never changes position. It is better to keep the timing of this exercise short than to allow your dog to break his position.
• When you are confident that your dog will not move, put him in the Sit in the Basic Position and leave his lead on the ground in front of him. Command him to "Wait" and go a pace or two in front of him. Count to ten and return.

The Wait is trained with the dog in Basic Position.

Photo: Steve Nash.

• Increase the duration until you are able to walk in a full circle around your dog with the lead lying on the ground.
• When your dog is solid in this exercise, start to introduce distractions, e.g., rustle paper, or ask someone to make noises or move around in the vicinity. Once again, start with small distractions and gradually increase these.
• Should the dog move at any time, return to him and place him back in the Sit, giving the correct commands. Go to the end of the lead in front of the dog and, very gently, pull on the lead repeating the "Sit" command. This has the effect of making the dog lock his body into the Sit position. Once your dog is totally confident in the Sit position, leave him at the "Wait". Then walk away, face him, and call him to you. Reward when he reaches you,

THE PRESENT ELEMENT
The Present is the next element to train.
• With your dog on a lead in front of you, and your feet slightly apart, gently encourage the dog into your body and command "Come". Use treats held high and close to your body, ensuring that you urge the dog into a straight position.
• Command "Sit" so that the dog ends up with his nose pointing up your body and his bottom in a straight line in front of you. If your dog does not come into a correct Present position, put your hands gently into his collar, under his chin, and gently draw him into the position making quite sure that he is absolutely straight, and that your hands are returned to the 'V' position before giving the Sit command. Reward (praise, treat), then release "Off" or "OK" and play.
• Take a pace or two back to the end of the lead. If your dog

The dog returns to the Present position.

Photo: Steve Nash.

is clearly coming in crooked, extend one foot so that he must come round that leg in order to get to you. This will help to straighten him out. Return your leg as soon as your dog has gone round it.

• Gradually increase the length of these recalls and once you are confident, remove his lead. As your dog progresses in this exercise you can start to introduce angled recalls so that he has to work harder to obtain the right position.

THE FINISH ELEMENT

The final element of the Recall exercise. With your dog on the lead in front of you, and the lead in your left hand, give the command "Close". There are then two methods. One is to:

• Encourage your dog round your right leg, with your right hand on the lead.

• Take a step forward with the left leg, at the same time bringing the dog round behind you into the Basic Position and commanding him to "Sit". Reward (praise, treat).

• Repeat this several times until the dog is coming round your legs happily. At this stage, you can drop the step forward and simply stand still.

• Do not, however, forget to encourage the dog with your right hand giving the signal to finish, your left hand on the lead, and your voice encouraging him at all times. Reward. Release and play.

The other method is known as the Continental Finish, and this involves calling your dog to heel, in a pivot in front of you, to the basic Position on your left side.

• Use the lead in your right hand.

The Finish: The dog goes behind the handler's legs to return to Basic Position.   Photos: Steve Nash.

• Put your left hand in the dog's collar while he swivels so that his turn is tight.
• Reward, and release "Off" or "OK".

RESPONSIBILITY
See Pack Leader page 165.

RETRIEVE
Your dog leaves your side to pick up an article you have thrown for him. He must pick it up cleanly without mouthing, return it to you straightaway, and give it to you on command.

TRAINING TECHNIQUES
As always, break the exercise down into its elements: Sit/Wait; Hold/Give; Outrun/Pick-up; Present and Give; Finish. Train them individually.
Sit/Wait: Command "Sit" with your pup by your left side. Use the aids (lead, voice). Command "Wait". Remember, however, that this is a separate element. Do not worry if he does not Wait in the excitement of his first Retrieves.
Hold/Give: Do not start teaching the Hold position when the pup is teething. Always use a soft article initially, e.g. the inside cardboard of toilet roll or an old sock with a knot in it.
• Start with your pup in the "Sit" position beside you. Show the pup the article and encourage him to take it. If he does so, give him the "Hold" command while he is holding the article firmly in his mouth. Do not allow your pup to spit the article out until you give the further command "Give".

• Use one hand to "Hold", and two for the "Give"
• Initially, do not expect the pup to "Hold" for more than a few seconds at a time. Once this is established, you can start to increase the time he holds the article. *Never* allow the pup to mouth (i.e. chew or chomp).
• Always offer the article with your hand at this stage. Do not expect your pup to pick up from the ground yet.
• Once your pup is happily taking the article from your hand, start to 'test' the Hold with one hand by gently tapping the end of the article and repeating the "Hold" command. If your pup shows any sign of mouthing or loosening his grip.
• Always take the article with both hands, very gently, using the command "Give". If you snatch the article you will encourage your pup to snatch back (the action/reaction principle), and before you know it you will have a dog that will not surrender the article to you without a fight. Before commencing teaching the Pick-up, you must be quite sure that your dog has been taught and understands the "Hold".

Outrun/Pick-up: Most puppies will chase an object that is thrown.
Train the Pick-up close to you, on the lead if needs be. Command "Hold" as before.

Present/Give: Train this element close to as part of the "Hold". Use two hands to take the article. Do not snatch.

Finish: This element is not essential, certainly in early training, but it is necessary in many competitions *(see Recall page 171)*.

The dog must wait in Basic Position while the dumb-bell is thrown.

Left: The out-run should be followed by a clean pick-up.

Above: The dog returns directly to the handler.

Right: Sitting in the Present, the dog gives up the dumb-bell on the command "Give".

PUTTING IT TOGETHER

The dog should go out and return at more or less the same pace. To achieve this, it is vital that the actual retrieve element should be separated from the control elements. It is recommend that you:-

• Do not insist on the "Wait" but rather hold your dog's collar while giving the "Wait" command. Excite the pup with your voice "Are you going to get it then?"..." What are you going to do?".

• Throw the article a reasonable distance. Let your dog go after the article, giving the "Hold" command.

• Command "Come" as soon as the dog has picked up the article and encourage him to come back fast and happily. If necessary, run away – this will speed him up! Do not insist on the Present yet as it will slow up his Recall. (This must be taught as a separate element).

• If the dog starts to mouth or chew the article, repeat the "Hold" element training totally apart from the actual retrieve.

• Play-retrieve with your dog, but do *not* give the "Hold" command.

REWARDS

Modern dog trainers use positive shaping and reinforcing behaviour by giving rewards for wanted actions.

WHAT ARE THEY?

A Reward can be almost anything that works – as in the Mafia expression "make him an offer he cannot refuse" Examples are:-

SENSE	REWARD
Hearing	Praise often overlooked, it must not be underestimated
	Reinforcers – Clicker, whistle, clapping etc.
Taste	Dog's meal can be divided
	Treats – Small food treats e.g. baked liver, cheese
Touch	Stroking, patting, etc.
Sight	Smile – You must look pleased
	Body Language – Show him how well he has done
Smell, Sight & Touch	Games, search, retrieve.

THEIR USE

Timing is vital. Your Reward must be immediately, instantaneously recognisable by your dog as related to the desired action.

Always reward for each successfully completed element (e.g. in Retrieve, train and reward each element of: the Wait; the Outrun; the Pick-up; the Hold; the Return and the Present), and until each is thoroughly learnt. When learnt, continue to Reward but randomly and unpredictably. This keeps your dog guessing and keen.

TRAINING TIPS
• Learn to use a conditioned reinforcer e.g. the instant "Good" voice command; a clicker; a whistle. This technique aids both your timing and the correct reinforcement of elements. For example, during a Retrieve click for a successful Outrun and for a successful Pick-up, but not for a poor Hold.
• Practise your timing. Make sure your treat/clicker is immediately available.
• Vary the rewards. Sometimes give treats, sometimes have a game, etc.
• Remember that properly timed Rewards are earned and just – they are not therefore bribery.

RING TRAINING
The art of showing a dog in competitions for breed.

There is a great deal more skill in this than may at first appear, and if you wish to show your dog you should join a club to learn these skills and to provide experienced people to 'go over' your dog to prepare him for the show ring.

WHAT IS REQUIRED?
When showing your dog in the breed ring you or your handler will be expected to show off your dog at a walk, trot, and in

A dog must be trained to 'gait' correctly in breed competition so the judge can assess movement and conformation.

Photo: Steph Holbrook.

some breeds, canter, on a loose lead, both in a straight line up and down from the judge and in a triangle so that the judge can assess your dog's front and back action.

Teach your dog the Basic Control position of Stand *(see page 190)* for a full examination (in some breeds this will be on a table). This will include a strange judge looking at his teeth, examining his body lines and feeling his rear end and tail set.

It is essential to show your dog to his best advantage. This requires knowledge and practice, together with an unbiased and critical assessment of your dog's good and bad points. Experienced handling can sometimes mean the difference between first place and no place at all.

ROLLING
Some dogs develop the distressing habit of rolling in muck, usually animal droppings – the juicier, stickier and nastier smelling the better. Cow and horse dung is comparatively harmless but fox, deer, skunk or dead fish can live with the dog and handler for a long time! What can be done?

SHAPING
As with so many habits, the best training is from puppyhood. Training is, of course, to shape the behaviour to show that rolling is unacceptable. Use the standard techniques.
• Basic training will teach "No" and "Leave". When successful, this should, of course, receive an instantaneous reward (click, treat, praise, etc.).
• Diversion – You must be more important than even the most attractive smell, and be able to recall your dog to come for a game or some other reward *(see page 178)* rather than roll.
   These techniques can and do work and many handlers have had great success with them.
• Aversion – Sound e.g. Discs, and/or Touch e.g. water *(see page 87)*

SCALE/SCALING WALL
This is an obstacle, usually 6 ft. high, for dogs to climb over in Working Trials, Police Trials, etc.

SCENT

Scent is the exercise where a dog uses his nose to find a correct (scented) article, usually one among many, discriminating it from others some of which are blank (unscented) and some are decoys (scented by others).

Scent is often a problem area for handlers usually due to unfortunate training. Every dog can scent. The most junior dogs in Working Trials who can find an article as small as a spark plug can certainly scent a huge white square in Obedience! You must train your dog to use his nose rather than his eyes, and to discriminate, i.e. reject, unwanted cloths.

TRAINING TECHNIQUES AND TIPS
• Hide toys first around the house and then in long grass. Command "Find".
• Train discrimination by using only two cloths (then progressively more), one with your (the handler's) scent, and the other scented by another. Fix these to a heavy board, tile, or similar so that they cannot be moved.
• Put salt on the reject cloths as a deterrent.
• As soon as the dog has the correct cloth, reward (praise, etc.). Later have the reward given by another handler.
• The exercise then becomes Retrieve. Train it as such.
• Do not rush your Scent training.

SEARCH

These are nosework exercises in which a dog finds articles (and humans), both in service work – for drugs, forensic, etc. and in sports (e.g. Working Trials, etc.)

The correctly scented article must be found from a series of unscented articles and decoys.   Photo: Steve Nash.

TRAINING TECHNIQUES
The training is similar to that of tracking.
• Show your dog articles, which you then hide, initially within an area well-known to the dog, and, later, in the great wide world. Train frequently.
• Later, do not show the articles to your dog. Just hide them.
• Practise close to you and then, when proficient, use a formal square. Walk round the square hiding the articles. Command "Find". Extend the size of the square.
• Put out more than the four articles required, even when you are practising, so that the dog is more assured of success. Pick up the others later.
• When the article is found, the exercise becomes a Retrieve and must be trained as such.
  Whether the Search is for an article in your sport, drugs, or a real-life criminal, always remember to reward for success.

SENDAWAY
The exercise is to train your dog to leave your side on command, and to proceed in a straight line in the direction indicated by you until you tell him to stop. The dog must stay in the designated spot until either recalled or redirected to another designated spot, before being recalled to you. Linked to the instantaneous "Down", it can be life-saving for your dog when close to traffic, sheep, etc.

TRAINING TECHNIQUES
While many trainers advocate that Sendaway training should not commence until the handler has trained the elements of "Wait" and an instant "Down", the modern view is that there is preliminary work that should be done with a pup from the earliest stages.
Phase 1: This training takes place at mealtimes.
• Put the food bowl at the end of a corridor. Hold your puppy at the other end.
• Let the puppy run to his food. Command "Go".
  Although the pup is intent on getting his food, nevertheless, repetition of the command will help shape his future performance. This procedure can be extended by putting the food bowl out in the garden, and giving the "Go" command over longer distances.
Phase 2: For next phase, enlist the help of a training companion.

- Each handler (but only one dog at a time) has a toy.
- The second handler keeps the dog by his side while the dog's own handler goes forward some ten paces. He exhibits the dog's toy and calls him.
- The first handler says "Go", the second handler says "Come". The dog runs between them. The second handler plays with the dog and then recovers the toy.
- Reverse the procedure.

It will readily be seen that this activity will be pleasurable to the dog and will be of help in training Recall as well as Sendaway. It also has the distinct advantage for us older handlers of allowing the pup to take a lot of exercise, pleasurable to him, without unduly tiring his handler!

Phase 3: For the third and more formal phase, the dog must now be able to perform the elements of "Wait" and instant "Down" (or "Sit") at a distance, on command. In this phase we build on the behaviour shaped in the first two phases. The equipment required is two poles (a wooden broom handle with a nail at the bottom and a couple of nails at the top is ideal).

- The handler, on his own or with his training companion, as appropriate, places one pole in the ground. He downs the dog by that pole.
- He then runs some ten to twenty yards away and plants a second pole. He calls the dog to him as a Recall. He downs him at the second pole.
- The handler then goes back to the first pole, and attaches a toy to the hook on the pole. He goes back to the other pole, sets the dog up with the command "Go".
- As soon as the dog (following his own body scent down the now well-worn, well-scented path) gets to the pole, " Down" him by the pole. You must run after your dog and reward him at the pole (with praise and play with the toy).

Phase 4: When the third phase has been thoroughly mastered, and the distance very gradually increased, the handler must

Train the Sendaway exercise through markers.

Photo: Steve Nash.

then find a fence or hedge, or some other barrier, against which to plant his pole in a particular spot.
• The procedure is as in Phase 3.
• It should soon be possible for the dog to recognise his spot without the aid of the pole.
• The distance must be increased gradually, ensuring that the dog thoroughly understands and enjoys the exercise at all distances.
• If there is any worry in the dog's mind (evidenced perhaps by looking around), the handler should go back one or more phases until the dog thoroughly understands.
Phase 5: This is redirection. A handler at this stage is beyond the scope of this book as it is a test of the most senior Working Trials class.

OBEDIENCE SENDAWAY
A dog who thoroughly understands Sendaways of 100 yards will have little problem in the much shorter Obedience Sendaways.

Refine your training for Obedience using a different set-up (the handler must stand up straight) and command "Away". Teach him the specific differences of going to a triangle, an end marker, a box, and through intervening markers.

It is recommended that you:
• Train the elements ("Wait", "Go", "Down", "Recall") separately.
• Train set-up. Turn the dog's head towards the target and shield his eyes so the dog looks straight. Use the command "Away" in Obedience, "Go" in Working Trials.
• Train the common Sendaway targets: box, triangle, back marker, through markers. Dogs are intelligent enough to learn the difference.
• Train for longer distance than required. Put up markers for the dog to go through. Then, when under Obedience test, the exercise is shorter and easier for your dog.

SETTLE
Settle is part of your Basic Control training *(see page 91)*. While not essential, it is certainly desirable behaviour.

Even the most senior competition dogs do no more than ten minutes of a formal Down-Stay, yet we want a pup to remain in one position often for much longer periods. The command "Settle" is used for this general quietness.

TRAINING TECHNIQUES
• After a meal, toilet training, and a game (so that he is tired) put your puppy in his crate. Command "Settle" each time he is put in his crate.
• Reward him always initially, later randomly when he responds. A chewy toy may help in the early stages.
• The puppy will soon learn to realise the crate is his own territory and will associate it with relaxation. Do not allow children – of any age – to fuss him when he is in his crate.
• Thereafter, practise outside the crate for progressively longer periods, then outdoors.
   Remember how many hours a day a dog sleeps. This is a relaxation exercise, not a formal "Stay" exercise.

SHEEPDOG TRIALS
These are specialised trials in which working sheepdogs compete against each other on a faults and time basis.

The skills learnt working on the farm are put to use in sheepdog trials.   *Photo: Keith Allison.*

The aim is to complete a specific herding operation at long range in as fast a time as possible. Dogs are marked on the outrun, pick up or fetch, the drive, the cross drive, the shed and the pen. The course will contain a number of hurdles or gates through which the handler must direct the dog to drive the sheep.
   Training sheepdogs for trials is a specialised activity. Contact the International Sheepdog Society for further details *(see Addresses page 208).*

SHOWS
If you are planning to enter your dog at a dog show held under national Kennel Club rules, you must follow the recognised procedure.

THE PROCEDURE
The procedure is covered in the Schedule/Premium list put out by the relevant show management.
• You must enter by the closing date on the correct form.
• You will be mailed a programme of judging which includes a timetable.
• When you arrive at the show, settle your dog and your belongings. Go to your ring and inform the Steward of that ring of your arrival.
• Ensure that your dog is comfortable, either in the car (with window opened and fresh water available to him) or, as is the case at some UK Breed shows, on his bench.
• Take your dog to the specified exercise area to relieve himself. Bag it and bin it.
   It is recommended that you:-
• Allow plenty of time to find your ring and, if possible, watch a segment of earlier judging.
• Do not trail your dog round the show with you all day. He will get hot and tired, and may not then perform at his best when required.
• If you leave your dog in your car, ensure it is shaded and ventilated. Fresh water must be available.
• Ensure that your dog has relieved himself before you enter the ring.
Enjoy your dog and your day, regardless of the outcome!!

SIRIUS
The Dog Star.

SIT
Sit is the Basic Control position where your dog has his rump on the ground, back legs tucked, with his front legs and trunk raised straight. Present is the Sit in front of the handler.

TRAINING TECHNIQUES
Sit is an essential exercise for all dogs. Train it positively, as soon as possible.

Sit by Side (The Basic Position):
• Start with your puppy on his lead. Guide him round to your left side with an instant reward (e.g. a treat), and the lead in your right hand.
• At the same time, push his rump down with your left hand whilst holding his head up with the lead and showing him the treat. Give the command "Sit".
• As soon as the puppy is sitting, give him the reward – treat, click, praise, etc.
• Relax him with "OK" or "Off".
• Increase the period of the Sit progressively before giving him his reward.
• Train "Sit" first on lead to your left side, and then off lead.
  Take time to ensure that the puppy understands and reacts instantly to your command. It is an essential element of many other exercises. If there is any doubt or delay, revert to puppy training.

Sit in Front (The Present)
This is the Sit directly in front of you. It is another essential exercise in Basic Control - and an element in other exercises. (Recall, Retrieve, etc.)
For training see Recall *(page 171)*, but briefly shape as before:-
• Kneel down to your puppy to get the right height (or sit in a chair).
• With your puppy on his lead, give his name and command "Come". Gently pull him towards you, showing him a treat.
• As he arrives in front of you, push down his rump with your left hand, raising his head gently on his lead with your right hand, holding the treat over his head.
• Command "Sit" and as soon as he sits, give him the treat.
• As before, increase the period of sitting progressively. Then train off the lead.

The Present can be trained with the handler sitting on a chair or a stool.

Photo: Brian McGovern.

Do not rush this exercise. Ensure that your puppy thoroughly understands it. When he does he will rush towards you both because of his reward (treat, click, praise, etc.) and because of the game.

SOCIALISATION
It is vital that your puppy learns to co-exist with other pack members, particularly children, dogs and other animals in the home, then other dogs and people outside the home.

Dogs must learn to co-exist with other animals.

It is also important for your puppy to become used to visitors to his territory (i.e. his home), particularly those carrying burdens, e.g., postmen, window cleaners, etc.
• You must introduce your puppy to visitors as they arrive.
• If you can, join a training club as soon as your pup has been vaccinated. It is helpful for dog and people socialisation outside the home. In many areas, socialisation classes (puppy parties) are organised, and these again are strongly recommended.

SOUND AVERSION
Aversion properly trained is an effective method of interrupting and then deterring unwanted behaviour. Sound aversion is based on the Pavlovian principle of conditioning reflex to noise.
See Aversion page 87.

S

SPEAK
"Speak" is the command for "Bark", and the name of the competition exercise. The objective is to get the dog to bark on command and stop barking on command.

When well-taught, the exercise is extremely beneficial for your pup, you and your family and friends. You will readily see that the dog that will bark on command will have its uses, whilst a dog that will stop barking on command will be greatly appreciated and, indeed, respected by the community! See Barking *(page 90)* for training techniques.

SPORTS
As man has striven for excellence in other areas and pursuits, so he has with the rearing and training of dogs for sporting purposes. He has sought to reach the pitch of perfection by having his dog shown to be the best whether as a breed specimen, as a trained individual competitor, or as part of a team.

The range of canine sports has expanded enormously in recent years, and there is a discipline to suit nearly all types and temperaments — human and canine. The most popular include:
Field Sports
• Hunting of fox, deer, hare, rats, mink, racoons, and many other species.
• Shooting, pointing and retrieving of game birds on land and from water.
• Drag hunting is now a popular option for hounds.
Racing Sports
• Coursing after hare has a long pedigree.
• Racing dogs against each other following an artificial lure, e.g. Greyhounds, Whippets, Lurchers, Terriers etc., is widespread.
• The sport of sled racing, using Huskies, has been developed in a number of countries.
Active Competitions
• Many competitions are based around the training programmes originally developed for working dogs. These include Sheepdog Trials, Police, Prison, and Bloodhound Trials. The increasingly popular sport of Agility is an off-shoot of training required by police and security dogs.
• Others are refined from the originals, e.g. Obedience, Working Trials, KCJO and some new, e.g. Flyball.

Breed sports
These are popular events worldwide. In the USA, the
American Kennel Club registers over 1.4 million purebred
dogs. In the UK the Kennel Club registers over 250,000
pedigree dogs. There are a number of shows for each of the
190 breeds recognised in Britain, culminating in the famous
'Supreme Champion' at Crufts each year, in the UK, while in
the US it is in 'Best in Show' at the prestigious Westminster
show held annually in Madison Square Garden New York
City.
New Sports
New sports are constantly being developed – Heelwork to
Music (UK)/Canine Freestyle (US) is a current example.
Some sports will be amended to become suitable for
international competition as quarantine laws are revised.
Similarly, some of the older sports will go into decline.
Illegal Sports
Public sentiment and modern legislation has changed
perception of what constitutes cruelty. A number of sports
have therefore been outlawed. They include bear baiting,
badger baiting, dog fighting, and, more recently, otter
hunting.

STAND
**Stand is the Basic Control position where your dog stands,
still, with all four feet on the ground. This position is
essential training and used not only in sports and
competitions, but also for grooming examination at the
vet, etc.**

TRAINING TECHNIQUES
• With the puppy in the Sit facing you, and a toy in your right
hand, pretend to throw the toy backwards over the pup's head.
The majority of pups will automatically jump backwards and
then stop in the Stand to look at the toy in your hand.
• Give his name and command "Back". ("Back" is used for
this command as "Stand" and "Sit" are too alike and are
easily confused, particularly at a distance in competition.)
• Reward with praise and throw the toy over his head. In the
early stages, only train the Back command occasionally. If
you attempt to 'trick' the pup too regularly he will cease to
react with the speed that you are aiming for. The important
thing is to make sure that the movement is never forwards.
• Once your pup is keenly responding to the "Back"

When the dog is sufficiently experienced, the Stand or "Back" can be trained as part of Distant Control.

Photo: Steve Nash.

command, encourage him to remain in that position for a short while with a "Wait".
• Build gradually on the time the puppy stays in position, rewarding each longer time, so that eventually the pup will maintain a comfortable "Back" position.

The training for the Stand-Stay is the same as for all other stays, once the Stand position has been comfortably established.

STAYS
The Sit and Down-Stay are essential Basic Control training, and the Stand is highly desirable.

TRAINING TECHNIQUES
Sit-Stay: Always start by training the Sit.
• With your dog on his collar and lead, encourage him into the Basic Position and give the command "Sit" firmly.
• At the same time, raise the lead above his head with your right hand and push down firmly but gently on his rump with your left hand.
• Reward him by praise or treat. Keep all rewards quiet and gentle when training the Stays.
• Ensure that the dog is sitting tidily with his feet neatly under him, and his tail out straight behind him. Do not let him lean on to your leg. As in Heelwork, his front feet should be level with your instep and his bottom exactly straight with your legs.
• Give the command "Stay", and holding the lead in your left hand above the dog's head, take a half pace away from him to

A group Stay: Despite the distraction of close proximity, these dogs are focused on the handler. Photo: Steve Nash.

the right, ensuring by use of the lead and your left hand that he does not move.

• Silently count to five, and then turn to the dog, praising him greatly but still ensuring that he does not move from the Sit position.

• Gradually increase the distance you move away from the dog: to his side, his front, and back, keeping him on the lead at all times and making quite sure that he never changes position. It is better to keep the timing of this exercise short than to allow the dog to break his position.

• When you are confident that your dog will not move, put him in the Sit in the Basic Position and, closing the loop of the lead on the ground in front of him, command him to "Stay" and go a pace or two in front of him. Count to ten and return.

• Again, increase the length of the exercise until you are able to walk in a full circle around your dog with the lead lying on the ground.

• Once your dog is solid in this exercise you should start to introduce distractions, e.g., rustle paper or ask someone to make other noises, or to move in the vicinity. Once again, start with small distractions and gradually increase them.

• Should your dog move at any time, return to him and place him back in the Sit giving the correct commands. Go to the end of the lead in front of the dog and very gently pull on the lead repeating the "Sit" command. This has the effect of making the dog lock his body into the Sit position.

• Once your dog is totally confident with distraction in the Sit position, and will maintain that position for three minutes without correction, you can very slowly begin to introduce the out of sight Sit. As with all other exercises, start with a very short time and distance and build up from there.

• Remember, that your dog needs to have total confidence in you before he will be able to bear you being out of his sight.

S

You must, therefore, be very understanding at this point.
• Never forget to reward him for his efforts.

Down-Stay: Once your dog is performing at least a one-minute Sit, you should have no problems with introducing the Down-Stay. The training is identical to the "Sit".
• With your dog on his collar and lead by your side, give the "Down" command. If necessary, encourage him into position with the treat between his front legs, and a firm but gentle push backwards and downwards on his shoulders using a cantilever action. Ensure that you do not hurt him.
• Thereafter, proceed as for the Sit, but remember that in time your dog will be required to perform a ten-minute Down out of sight.

Stand-Stay: Once your dog is entirely confident in the Sit and the Down, you can start to introduce the Stand. Initially, it is important to remember that the Stand position is one of dominance and, therefore, it is better to teach this exercise in isolation so that your dog is not intimidated by other dogs in the early stages of his training.
• With your dog on his collar and lead, gently encourage him into the Stand position with the "Back" command. See Stand *(page 190)* but briefly:-
• Pretend to throw a toy over the dog's head.
• As he jumps into position, reward him.
• Once in position, encourage the dog to remain there by stroking his back and pushing down gently in the middle of his back, whilst repeating the "Back" command. This will make him lock his legs and have the effect of making him much more stable in this position.
• Thereafter, proceed as for the "Sit".

STRAYING
Some dogs have a tendency to stray away from home, and this must be stopped at an early stage to avoid calamity.

TACKLING THE PROBLEM
There are three ways to tackle this problem:
Basic Control Training: Basic training, which all dogs must receive, should emphasise response to the dog's name, Recall to handler, the instant "Down" etc. When these become ingrained, it will inhibit straying while the dog is under the control of the handler. *See Basic Control page 91.*
Diversion: The handler is pack leader and must make himself the most interesting object in the park, and in the

neighbourhood, so that the dog would rather return to the handler for rewards or games or other diversions, than stray off on his own, doing 'his own thing'. *See Diversion page, 122.*

Aversion: If basic training and diversion have failed, then the Aversion techniques *(see page 87)* may be employed including the use of noise (tin can or discs).

PREVENTION

Some handlers who struggle to prevent straying, protect their pets and, indeed, themselves by fencing their property or confining the dog in a kennel and run. The electronic fence can be used to great effect. *(See Containment pages 114)*

Outside the home, the dog is kept on the lead, and in this instance, the flexi-lead gives a greater degree of freedom.

If all these techniques have been employed and failed, then the owner still has a duty to his dog and to himself. He must ensure that the dog has collar and tag. If the dog is a notorious strayer who manages to lose his collar, then either tatooing or microchiping is an essential. *See Identification, page 153.*

SWIMMING
Many dogs love water: paddling in it, playing in it, swimming, and retrieving from it. All dogs can swim. However, while many dogs take to water naturally, others do not. In the case of working gundogs or police dogs, who must cross water on command, training may be required to overcome an initial reluctance.

TRAINING TECHNIQUES
Any diffidence with regard to entering water must be overcome by positive behaviour shaping. Start training near a smooth stretch of water with a gentle sloping bank.
• Encourage the dog to walk around in the shallow water on a lead followed by a reward (treat, game, praise, etc.).
• If the dog is still reluctant, the handler must, heroically,

Breeds such as the Labrador Retriever, are generally great swimming enthusiasts.

paddle in to encourage the dog and build up confidence.

• When the dog is in the water, encourage him to retrieve suitable floating objects thrown by the handler. Such articles may be a floating dummy, plastic bottle, appropriate balls, sticks, etc.

• Training can be developed further by gradually increasing the distance and the depth of water in which the object is thrown. This will almost always result in the dog swimming without difficulty.

FIRST AID

Hopefully, you will have chosen a safe spot for your dog to swim, but if your dog does get into difficulties in the water, this is what action you should take:

• Get the dog on to dry land, then hold him by his two rear legs, head downwards, at a sufficient height to allow the water in his lungs and stomach to pour out through his nose and mouth.

• When this water stops running, lay the dog down and commence artificial respiration.

• Kneel by the side of the dog and parallel to it; apply pressure to the dog's chest cavity and, if appropriate, give mouth to mouth resuscitation.

TABLE

A table is a useful aid for training and other interaction. The use of a table or other raised area is helpful in Basic Control training, for grooming, and for examination by the vet. It is also an essential part of an Agility course.

TRAINING TECHNIQUES

• Initially lift the pup on to the table giving the command "Up".

• Use an intermediate box as a step and encourage the pup to jump up on it to the table, with the lure of a treat and reward. Command "Up" and then "Wait". Reward.

• Increase the time that the dog spends stationary on the table.

• Ensure that there is no problem with inspecting him for grooming, etc.If necessary, train this element separately on the level.

The Table is used as an exercise in Agility competition.

Photo: Keith Allison.

• Teach him to go "Down" on the table. This is a useful control exercise (it is essential to teach a dog to go "Down" in a variety of circumstances as a safety measure). It is a specific exercise in the sport of Agility.

It is recommended that you:
• If your dog is reluctant to get on to the table, climb on to it yourself, in the kneeling position, and call the dog up to you.
• When the dog has come to the Recall, give him his Reward. Get him to Wait while you dismount. It will then be simple to teach him to go Down on the table from the Sit.
• Use the table for inspection and grooming, particularly since it saves not only the vet's back, but also your own!

TERRITORY
A dog like any other pack animal is a territorial animal. A dog will naturally protect his territory including his perceived territory. This will include his own den, his wider den (your house), his moving den (the car), and other areas.

It is important to draw firm guidelines for yourself and your dog as to what constitutes acceptable territorial defence and what does not. Obviously, as pack leader, you must have access to all areas. If the dog will not allow you to have access to any part of your home, stairs, etc., you must change his attitude by a dominance reshaping programme. See Dominance *(page 125)*, but briefly: -
• You must enter your dog's bed, sleeping area, etc. He must not enter yours.
• You must have access to all chairs, sofas, etc. Do not allow your dog to claim any one as his own.
• Do not allow him to occupy strategic areas of the house which will mean that you and other senior members of the

pack have to go round him. These areas include doorways, stairways, etc. You must make the dog move out of your way and not the reverse. Do not apologise when you walk through him. He must apologise to you!

• Do not forget your Basic Control training *(page 91)* even when your dog is adult. Your five-minute session a day will help him, and will reinforce his position in your pack.

THERAPY DOGS

Therapy dogs provide caring community service to people who miss animals in their lives and focus attention on the physical and psychological benefits which dogs can provide.

Therapy dog charities have been developed in many countries, and there are now thousands of volunteers who help. Dogs are required to pass a temperament test, and, of course, to have had Basic Control training.

Examples of Therapy dogs in practice are visits by the dog and handler to hospitals, senior citizens' homes and other similar institutions. Patients benefit by contact with stroking, fondling and otherwise talking to the dogs.

While some of these Therapy dogs have been highly trained (they include a well-known Crufts Obedience Championship winner), they can and do come from all levels of training. Providing the dog can pass the temperament test and has good Basic Control training, he will be acceptable.

It is recommended that you help with this work since it provides an extension of your training and also helps people in need. It fosters good relations between the dog and the community. For further details see Addresses *(page 208)*.

THUNDER
See Noise Tolerance page 162.

TOYS
See Games page 138.

TRACKING
Tracking is a canine activity wherein the dog, ahead of its handler, follows a track (usually human) accurately. It is used in the civil services (police, prison, taxation etc.) and in several sports.

TRAINING TECHNIQUES

As with all such activities and sports, it is essential for a beginner to get the right start. There is nothing more frustrating for handler and dog than to have to unlearn bad habits. This is considerably more difficult than learning correctly in the first place. There are now good books available on this single subject.

As always train your dog by breaking the exercise into its component elements.

Articles: Train your dog to be fanatical about articles. The track is the means to finding articles. Encourage him to find and then play with them.

• Show the article to your dog indoors and then hide it in the house. When he finds it, reward him, preferably with vigorous play with that article. For this purpose use a length of thick rope, rubber hose, or a ball on a rope.

• Extend the game to the garden and then further afield.

Finding articles after a search is the foundation both of tracking and the search square. Although the articles may be large, such as a hosepipe or ball, they must be hidden. The dog is being taught to use his nose on the ground so that it is a scent and not a sight test.

Control: The majority of dogs love tracking, but their natural enthusiasm must be channelled to ensure that they do not overrun corners or take the track at such a speed that they miss the articles which may be both small and hidden.

• Do not allow your pup to yaw wildly from side to side or charge at the full extent of the 30 ft line so that he overshoots corners.

• Do not be the novice handler using the line like a wild west cowboy practising with a lariat!

Early tracking: It is helpful to have either another handler to hold your pup or a post to tie him to.

• Lay the first track by putting a toy – the hose-pipe or the ball on the rope – at the end of a lead or line. Drag the toy on

In training, the track is seen as a means to finding 'toys'.

Photo: Keith Allison.

the ground behind you. Show it to your dog throughout, and keep his attention on it until you hide the toy.

• Rush back to your dog, affix a double lead, and later the harness, and encourage him to "Find".

• When he does find an article, reward with praise, treat, and with his toy.

• When your dog is one hundred per cent certain of this game, extend the track gradually from 20 yards up to 50 yards.

• It is prudent to put down an extra article. This is not so that your pup retrieves both, but to ensure that he will always be successful in his search. Even if he goes over the first hidden article, he should meet the second. If he meets the first, you should go up later and retrieve the second yourself.

Corners and Curves: Only move to corners when you and your dog are fully proficient with straight tracks of differing lengths, working up to around 100 yards and always recovering the article.

• Start with a right-angled turn. Lay a short 30-yard track up to a hedge or wall.

• Turn right for 25 yards. Triple-lay (i.e., go back to the turn and back again). Hide three articles.

• Only progress to left angles, then acute and obtuse angles, and, eventually, curves when your dog is proficient at the earlier stages.

Track-laying: Modern teaching suggests that handlers lay their own training tracks. While it is true that in competition the tracks are laid by strangers, competitions will be the exception rather than the rule. Only the occasional practice track should be laid by a stranger.

The reason for this is simple. To ensure the accuracy that is essential, the handler needs to know precisely both where the articles have been hidden and where the turns are. Track-laying is in itself a skill. Novice handlers may wish to make use of tracking poles to indicate where there are corners as well as natural markers like clumps of bushes, trees, etc.

Unless you know *exactly* where the track is, neither you nor your dog will be sure what is happening. All that will actually happen is that error will be reinforced for the future. Practise track-laying without your dog. Only when you can remember where the articles were hidden and can recover them yourself should you proceed with your dog.

TRAFFIC
Uncontrolled dogs can cause accidents in traffic. Vehicles

can kill your dog. Train your dog positively to accept the rush and noise of traffic.

Position your dog by your side in the Basic Position on his collar and lead. As always, train in short sessions. If your dog is noise sensitive, follow a Noise Tolerance programme *(see page 162)* before exposing him to traffic. Keep your dog on his collar and lead at all times, and remember that you must control him in traffic.

TRAVEL
See Car And Travel page 101.

TRAINING
See Basic Control page 91.

TRESPASS
A dog which is on property where it has no right to be, or where its owner has no right or permission to allow it to be, is trespassing.

If during the trespass the dog kills or injures livestock, the keeper of the dog is liable. Not only the owner, but also the keeper, may be prosecuted for the offence of 'worrying livestock'. This includes attacking or, chasing them so as to cause them injury or suffering. Even being in a field or enclosure in which there are sheep when the dog is not on a lead, or otherwise under close control, is an offence. You may also be sued in a civil court for damage done.

Keep your dog under strict control at all times so that there is no possible risk of criminal prosecution or civil litigation.

U

UP
"Up" is the command for your dog to jump up on the grooming table, veterinary table or jump obstacles in competition. It can also be used for getting into the car.
See Table (page 195) for training

VIDEO
A video camera and recorder can be a useful aid in training dogs.

A video can be used in two key areas:-
• If there is a training problem that the handler cannot resolve, a video taken by a third party, may give clues to the handler and certainly to the instructor or behaviourist as to the cause of the problems, and therefore, hopefully, to the solutions.
• A video of a dog in competition, whether it be Obedience, Agility, or any other discipline, is of immense benefit both to the competitor and to his trainer or instructor for planning a subsequent training programme.

VOCABULARY
It is amazing how much a well-trained dog can understand of human vocabulary, proving how intelligent and adaptable canines can be.

The dog's understanding can be divided into the following areas:
Tone: A dog listens to his handler's tone more than to his individual words. A handler can tell a dog that he is a "bad dog" in a loving tone and the dog will wag his tail. Similarly, you can tell a dog that he is a "good dog" in a gruff tone, and the dog will cower.
Signals: A handler's body language sends out massive signals to a dog. A dog is much more sensitive than humans to body language. Humans can tell whether a team has been victorious in a football game by looking at the body language of the two sides. Those with their heads erect and the smiles and air punching have won, those with their heads down and dragging feet have lost. A dog can differentiate not only this but also much, much more.

Arising from body language are deliberate signals by the handler using his head, hand, leg, etc. For example, an extended arm is used to redirect left or right.

An interesting application of this was when I succeeded in retraining an old dog who had become deaf. He had already learnt distance control exercises with verbal commands, but

The whistle is used when training working sheepdogs, and also for gundogs in the field.

Photo: Steve Nash

this was adapted so he could do the same exercises relying on hand signals without words. The hand signals merely changed the dog's vocabulary.
See Body Language page 97.
Noise: The clicker, tin-cans or discs, the whistle, and for hounds alone, the whip, are all noise communications. Used correctly, each is a communication from handler to dog with a positive or negative meaning.
Voice: Voice commands are vital. This is because the human handler understands their import. To the dog it does not matter whether the voice vocabulary is English or Swahili. What is vital is that the same word/sound is used to obtain a required reaction.

Ideally, the words must be monosyllabic, e.g. "Come", "Sit", etc. Each word must be clear to both handler and dog, and should only be used in that required context. It is totally confusing to an albeit willing dog to be told one time to "Sit", another time to be told "Down", and then to be told "Sit down" when the handler wants nothing more than Sit.

In addition to the handler always using the same words, you must ensure that all others in his pack – all family members – must use precisely the same words and/or signals. Keep a list of words or signals for your dog's actions that is accessible to every member of your human pack (and your dog's instructor).
See Commands, page 113.

WAIT
Wait is one of the essential Basic Control exercises (*see page 91*). Your dog must remain in the position you specify until you call him to you.

TRAINING TECHNIQUES

• Place your dog in the Basic Position Sit *(see page 92)* – "Sit".

• Ensure that he is sitting tidily with his feet neatly under him and his tail out straight behind him. Do not let him lean on to your leg. As in Heelwork, his front feet should be level with your instep and his bottom exactly straight with your legs.

• Give the command "Wait" Hold the lead in your left hand above the dog's head, and take a half pace away from him to your right, ensuring by use of the lead and your left hand that he does not move.

• Silently count to five, and then return to your dog. Praise him, but ensure that he does not move from the Sit position.

• Gradually increase the distance you leave your dog to the side, the front and the back, keeping him on the lead at all times. Make sure that he never changes position. It is better to keep the timing of this exercise short than to allow the dog to break his position.

• When you are confident that the dog will not move, put him in the Sit in the Basic Position, and, closing the loop of the lead on the ground in front of him, command him to "Wait". Move a pace or two in front of him. Count to ten and return.

• Again, increase the time until you are able to walk in a full circle round your dog with the lead lying on the ground.

• When the dog is solid in this exercise, start to introduce distractions, e.g., rustle paper or ask someone to make other noises, or move in the vicinity. Once again, start with small distractions and gradually increase these.

• Should the dog move at any time return to him and place him back in the Sit. Go to the end of the lead in front of the dog and, very gently, pull on the lead repeating the "Sit" command. This has the effect of making the dog lock his

When training "Wait", gradually increase the distance you leave the dog.

Photo: Keith Allison.

203

body into the Sit position. Walk backwards 3-5 paces and call him to you. Reward.
• Extend the time of the Wait, and the distance you leave your dog, gradually.

WATCH
See Basic Position page 92.

WESTMINSTER
Westminster is the most prestigious dog show held in the United States. It is held annually in Madison Square Garden in New York City. It is broadly equivalent to Crufts in the UK and attracts many visitors both from the US and from overseas.

It has been referred to as the Champions Breed Show because only purebred dogs which have won their Championship in the United States are eligible for entry.

The show started in 1877 and is now a two-day event held in February. Although the show deals only with Breed competition, there is also a class for junior handlers aged between 10-16 years. This is known as Junior Showmanship. The handlers are judged solely on their handling ability and compete for the coveted title of "International Junior Handler of the Year".

WORKING TRIALS
Working Trials is a sport in the USA and UK. While its major part is nosework, it covers a wide spectrum of exercises.

Working Trials embrace tests of: -
• Nosework a) Recovering small articles from a track, up to three hours old, of up to 1,000 yards, with corners, bends, etc. b) Search square - recovering four articles hidden in a 25 yard square.
• Agility (6 ft scale/scaling wall, clear jump and long jump).
• Control (Heelwork, Sendaway, Recall, Retrieve, Speak, Noise tolerance and Stays).

Dogs progress through stages which also act as a handicap system to encourage the less experienced dogs. At each stage there is an Open Trial at which one or more qualifications must be obtained and thereafter a Championship Trial. Having obtained appropriate qualifications at each stage at the

Championship Trial the dog is entitled to post the appropriate initials with EX (Excellent) after his name, like University degrees.

There is a small group of civilian handlers who compete for the PD (Patrol Dog) Finals. PD is not covered here, as handlers will have progressed far beyond the realms of this book

NOSEWORK
See Search page 181; Tracking page 197.

AGILITY
Working Trials Agility consists of three jumps. The long jump of 9 ft over five elements, the clear jump of 3 ft and a scale of 6 ft. Your club will have this equipment. Beginner handlers must not train on these jumps without a competent instructor.

These exercises are regarded with some trepidation by beginner handlers. There is a fear that dogs may injure themselves. However, discussions with vets have shown that there should be no problem to the dog who is properly trained. The proof of this pudding is in its eating. There are no more injuries to Working Trials Agility dogs than other dogs.
• Train by reward using praise and a toy.
• For each of the three jumps use the element "Wait", wave the toy to attract your dog's attention. Place the toy either over the A-frame at the end of the long jump or show it to him over the Scale.
• Return to the dog and send him over the obstacle with the command "Over" to get his reward, then the "Down" (or "Sit") element on the other side before you rejoin your dog.

A constant set-up for each obstacle is advised. Some recommend the same distance away as the obstacle is high or long. For the scale/scaling wall, where the dog has to set off within 9 ft of the obstacle, a distance of two paces (approx. two yards) is ideal. For the long jump, many handlers use five paces (to give five yards, including one taking off and one landing), and for the clear jump, a single pace. Other handlers have a longer or shorter run. Find which is best for your dog and stick to it.

Training for each of the jumps must be in easy stages. Break it up into its elements, and see Agility *(page 76)*.
The Long Jump: Keep the sections close together initially

The Long Jump.

Photo: Steve Nash.

(approx. 4 ft 6 ins to 5 ft), with a toy some yards away from the end. You can also put tracking poles, visible to the dog, to the left and right of the end section to avoid him going off at a tangent.

• Use the "Wait" element, then "Over".
• Use the "Down"/"Sit" element on the other side.
• Extend only when the dog is confident.
• Train the elements separately. Avoid formality at first until the dog understands.

The Clear Jump: Train initially with the pole at approx. 2 ft 6 ins. It is also helpful in training to make the hurdle solid by putting a cloth over it so it appears to be a solid barrier rather than the single bar that it actually is.

• Use the "Wait" element, then show the toy and throw it to the other side.
• Command "Over".

The Scale/Scaling wall: Start training with an A-frame. Each club will have one of these. It will be progressively steepened during training. When it has reached approx. 4ft 6 ins or 5 ft (depending on the dog), you can move on to the vertical Scale itself, with the top plank at no more than 4 ft. The plank should be added gradually until the full height is reached.

• Only when the dog is going over one way comfortably should the Recall be introduced.
• Only when going over and the Recall is solid should you introduce formality ("Wait", etc.)

CONTROL

For training of each of the exercises see Heelwork *(page 146)*, Sendaway *(page 182)*, Retrieve *(page 175)* , Recall *(page 171)* , Stays *(page 191)* and Noise tolerance *(page 162)*. Some specifics:-

• The gun should now be trained specifically (a cap gun initially, and your club will have a blank firing revolver), as before by the handler's side using the aids.
• Only when secure, leave the dog in a different position "Down", etc., extending distance gradually.

Heelwork: Although similar to a precision Obedience round (no commands and slow, normal and fast paces), it differs from it because:

• The emphasis is placed on a natural manner, so swing both arms.

• Less precision is required because of the rough terrain.

Speak: *See Barking page 90.*

X BREEDS
Cross breeds may be deliberately bred (e.g. collie/retriever) or accidental (mongrels).

In many countries, including the USA, most canine competitions are limited to registered purebred (pedigree) dogs. In the UK, only pedigree dogs can enter breed shows, but cross breeds are allowed to participate in sports competitions (e.g. Obedience, Agility, Flyball, Working Trials) if they are on the UK Kennel Club register.

The issue of purebred/mongrel will be addressed further when the various national authorities reach agreement on the rules for international competitions.

YOU AND YOUR DOG
You and your dog are the most important elements in dog training. Remember you are a team. Enjoy your time together.

ZEST
Zest is the enthusiasm that you put into training your dog.

You are his pack leader: he enjoys games with you and the quality time you spend with him. Every handler can find at least five minutes a day, and a square yard or two of floor space to work toegther.

Use this time to reinforce his shaping:

• Do Basic Control training. Vary the elements/exercises, e.g.
• Use the dog's name, then Recall/Finish.
• Command Sit, Down or Stand.
• Take one pace, then practise turns (Left, Right, About).
• Vary the order. Practise Retrieve, Leave.
• Remember to reward success, always at first, randomly thereafter.

It is only five minutes a day – and it is for your beloved dog!

APPENDIX: ADDRESSES

KENNEL CLUBS
United States
American Kennel Club, 5580 Centerview Drive, Raleigh, NC 27606.
United Kennel Club, 100 East Kilgore Street, Kalamazoo, MI 49001.
Canada
Canadian Kennel Club, 89 Skyway Avenue, Suite 100, Etobicoke, Ont, Canada M9W 6R4.

United Kingdom
The Kennel Club, 1, Clarges Street, Piccadilly, London, W1Y 8AB.
Australia
Australian National Kennel Council, PO Box 285, Red Hill South, Victoria 3937, Australia.

WELFARE
United States
American Humane Association (AHA), 63 Inverness Drive, E., Englewood CO 80112-5117
American Society for the Prevention of Cruelty to Animals (ASPCA) 441 E. 92nd Street, New York, 10128
Humane Society of the United States, 2100 L Street NW, Washington, DC 20037
The Seeing Eye Inc., PO Box 375, Morristown, New Jersey, 07963-0375
Therapy Dogs International, 6 Hilltop Road, Mendham, NJ 07945

United Kingdom
RSPCA Causeway, Horsham, West Sussex, RH12 1HG
National Canine Defence League 17, Wakeley Street, London EC1V 7LT
People's Dispensary for Sick Animals Whitechapel Way, Priorslee, Telford, Shropshire TF2 9PO
International Sheep Dog Society, Chisam House, Bromham Road, Bedford, MK40 2AA.
Guide Dogs for the Blind Association Hillfields, Burghfield, Reading, Berks. RG77 3YG
Hearing Dogs for the Deaf London Road, Lewknor, Oxon, OX9 5RY
Pets as Therapy (PAT dogs/PRO dogs), Rocky Bank, 4, New Road, Ditton, Maidstone Kent ME20 6AD
Association of Pet Behaviour Counsellors, PO Box 46, Worcester, WR8 9YS
Dogs for the Disabled The Old Vicarage, London Road, Ryton-on-Dunsmore, Coventry CV8 3ER.
W.F. Smith & Co., Solicitors, Glencoe House, 25, Market Place, Dereham, Norfolk. NR19 2AX.